T0358785

Praise for

Makini Howell

and

Makini's Vegan Kitchen

"We so appreciate the wonderfully creative recipes in this very beautiful cookbook! The importance of delicious vegan food helps pave the way for those who desire to make the transition from the standard animal-based diet."

—Joaquin Phoenix, Academy Award–nominated actor and activist,
Summer Phoenix, Rain Phoenix, and Liberty Phoenix

"The food at Plum Bistro is comfort food, fresh food, tasty and innovative food: a testament to the talented and driven owner and head chef, Makini Howell. It's one of my favorite vegan restaurants in the world."

—India.Arie, Grammy Award–winning singer-songwriter

"What Makini does at Plum and as a personal chef is creative, innovative, and satisfying. . . . Instead of seeing 'vegan' as a restriction, she has her own style. I never feel like I am missing anything."

—Common, Grammy Award–winning actor, author, artist, and activist

"I dare you to open this cookbook from Seattle's Plum Bistro to any page and *not* think the recipe you find there is completely irresistible. Tiramisu pancakes? Check. Cauliflower bisque with fresh fennel? Yes, please. Black plum and ginger sorbet? Oh, you know it. Chef Makini Howell's recipes are vibrant, wholesome, and absolutely popping with all the fresh flavors of the season. . . . Oh, and did I mention they're all vegan?"

—The Kitchn

"From Seattle food icon Makini Howell comes this much-anticipated cookbook, a luscious volume of recipes from the author's family-owned restaurant, Plum Bistro. Howell's cooking is all about simple, fresh, and local, and this photo-filled book . . . showcases such delights as Pesto Plum Pizza, Barbecue Oyster-Mushroom Sliders, and Fresh Blueberry Shortcake. Let the mouthwatering commence."

—*VegNews*

SIMPLE GOODNESS

ALSO BY MAKINI HOWELL

Makini's Vegan Kitchen: 10th Anniversary Edition of the Plum Cookbook

SIMPLE GOODNESS

NO-FUSS, PLANT-BASED MEALS STRAIGHT FROM YOUR PANTRY

MAKINI HOWELL

with Chef Marcos Pineda

Photography by Elizabeth Rudge
Prop Styling by Jenn Elliott Blake
Food Styling by G. Tyler Hill

hachette
BOOKS
New York

Note: The information in this book is true and complete to the best of our knowledge. This book is intended only as an informative guide for those wishing to know more about health issues. In no way is this book intended to replace, countermand, or conflict with the advice given to you by your own physician. The ultimate decision concerning care should be made between you and your doctor. We strongly recommend you follow their advice. Information in this book is general and is offered with no guarantees on the part of the authors or Hachette Go. The authors and publisher disclaim all liability in connection with the use of this book. The names and identifying details of people associated with events described in this book have been changed. Any similarity to actual persons is coincidental.

Cover design by Amanda Kain
Cover photo by Elizabeth Rudge

Hachette Go, an imprint of Hachette Books
Hachette Book Group
1290 Avenue of the Americas
New York, NY 10104
HachetteGo.com
Facebook.com/HachetteGo
Instagram.com/HachetteGo

First Edition: December 2024

Published by Hachette Go, an imprint of Hachette Book Group, Inc. The Hachette Go name and logo is a trademark of the Hachette Book Group.

Hachette Go books may be purchased in bulk for business, educational, or promotional use. For information, please contact your local bookseller or Hachette Book Group Special Markets Department at special.markets@hbgusa.com.

The publisher is not responsible for websites (or their content) that are not owned by the publisher.

Print book interior design by Diahann Sturge-Campbell

Library of Congress Cataloging-in-Publication Data

Names: Howell, Makini, author.
Title: Simple goodness : no-fuss, plant-based meals straight from your pantry / Makini Howell.
Description: First edition. | New York, NY : Hachette Go, 2024. | Includes index.
Identifiers: LCCN 2024001640 | ISBN 9780306829987 (hardcover) | ISBN 9780306829994 (epub)
Subjects: LCSH: Vegan cooking. | LCGFT: Cookbooks.
Classification: LCC TX837 .H698 2024 | DDC 641.5/6362—dc23/eng/20240216
LC record available at https://lccn.loc.gov/2024001640

ISBNs: 978-0-306-82998-7 (hardcover), 978-0-306-82999-4 (ebook)

Printed in China

IMG

10 9 8 7 6 5 4 3 2 1

To my beloved Baba,

It was such a place of deep love and belonging for me growing up as your daughter. Your unwavering faith, care, and guidance gave me the courage to become the woman I am today. If I could talk to you one more time, I would tell you so many stories. Some funny and some completely outrageous, and I know we would talk for hours just like we always did. Your homegoing has left my heart broken. But when I think of the lessons in faith, trust, and courage, I think of the times you would encourage me to leap through the air from the top steps of our house with only the faith that you would catch me.

It was such an adventure watching you chase down your own courage with the risk you took and the way you believed wholeheartedly in anything you dedicated yourself to, much like your journey into veganism and your passion for societal change. I remember when you determined that we would be vegan, taking us through the backwoods of Alabama to find tempeh somewhere deep in the South, and that same southern backyard of ours smelling of pit smoke and the sounds of roots reggae music playing with lyrics of love and brotherhood of man drifting through the air as you smoked tofu to perfection with such excitement for the deliciousness you and Mom created.

So much of you was about finding the goodness in the places where you found yourself or with the things you did and the people you knew. Your energy filled life with an amazing forward trajectory full of courage, commitment, adventure, fun, and constant good food. You had to have been the most forward-thinking and believing person I have ever met; you were so far ahead of your time, and knowing you was such a gift.

From you I learned how to carry a purpose forward in life. I have learned how to find the goodness in the places I find myself and with the people I know. Being your daughter taught me the power of forgiveness and grace. The unwavering love of a southern faith-filled father is a powerful thing, and I am grateful I got to experience it. It's hard to put into words what you have given me, but you have left me with a purpose in my heart and a deep caring in my spirit.

Thinking of you reminds me of Corinthians 13. It starts out "Love is patient, love is kind," and for me, having grown up as your daughter, faith and hope hold some of the deepest meanings in that verse, but the greatest of all is love. To have been loved by you was the gift of my life.

Thank you, Baba.

Kai

Marinara
Veggie Stock
Vegan Chicken Stock

Contents

Foreword by Stevie Wonder xv
Introduction: What Is Simple Goodness? 1
Stocking Your Kitchen for a Plant-Based Life 4

Simply Good Flavor Staples 11

Jalapeño Dip 12
Dill Dip 12
Chipotle Dip 13
Papa's Sammie Sauce 13
Tabasco Aioli 14
Tajín Butter 14
Yogurt Tahini Sauce 15
Fresh Cilantro Pesto 15
Black Pepper Breading 16
Mild Black Pepper Breading 16
Panko Breading 17
Taco Seasoning 17
Vegan Ranch 18
Buffalo Sauce 18
Sweet Chili Sauce 19
Marinara Sauce 19
Fresh Herb Oil 20
Sun-Dried Tomato Sammie Relish 20
Bacon Bits and Bacon Oil 21
Bacon Vinaigrette 22
Burger Seasoning 22
Sautéed Onions 23
Special Sauce 23
Wedged Roasted Yams 24
Spanish Rice 24
Pico de Gallo 25
Pepper Pot Pickled Onions 25
Red Cabbage Lime Slaw 26
Fresh Coriander Vinaigrette 26
Veggie or Vegan Chicken Stock 27
Gyro Spice Blend 28
Parmesan Herb Croutons 29
Strawberry Skillet Jam 30
Box Cornbread/Muffins 30
Pimiento Cheese 31
Coconut Cheesecake Butter 32
Sweet Skillet Southern Fried Apples 32
Plain Chia Pudding 33
Garlic Bread 33
Everyday Italian Salad 34
Tostones 35
Tangy Skillet BBQ Beans 36

Good Morning Goodness 37

Weekday Breakfast

The Incredible Hulk 39
Orange Sunrise 41
Strawberry Chia Power Smoothie 43
The Blacker the Berry . . . 45
Costa Rican Rice and Bean Bowl 47
Baba's Morning Quinoa 49
Fruity Chia Yogurt Bowls with Toasted Granola 51

Weekend Breakfast
Good Morning Breakfast Tacos 53
Bacon and Scrambled Egg Tacos 53
Spicy Sausage and Hash Browns Tacos 54
Plant Beef and Cheese Taquitos with Queso Sauce 55
Sunday Morning Celebration 57
Salted Caramel French Toast with Skillet Spiced Apples 57
Tofu Egg Scramble 58
Skillet Breakfast Potatoes 59
Breakfast Sausage 60
Southern Saturday Morning 63
Pan-Fried Eggs 63
Tofu Bacon or Tempeh Bacon 64
Grits and Grease 64

Simple Lunches and Anytime Meals 65
Citrus Black-Eyed Pea Salad with Sweet Cornbread 67
Middle Eastern–Inspired Chickpea Salad with Grilled Pita 69
Calamari Lettuce Wraps 71
General Tso Cauliflower 72
Savory Egg Pancake with Napa Cabbage Slaw and Steamed Rice 75
Napa Cabbage and Julienned Cucumber Quick Slaw 77
Hello Sunshine Quinoa Tabbouleh 79
Roasted Red Pepper Soup 81
French Onion Soup with Herby Cheese Toast 83
Crockpot Louisiana-Style Gumbo 85
Roasted Mushroom Bisque with Herby Cheese Toast 87
Cauliflower and Yam Bisque 89
Blackened Tofu Grinders 90
Bacon and Egg Grinder 92
Portobello Gyros 95
Tofu Bacon, Lettuce, and Tomato Sammie 97

Everyday Suppers 99
Wild Mushroom Ragù with Parmesan Gnocchi 101
Eggplant Parmesan with Alfredo Rigatoni and Lemon Olive Oil Arugula 103
The New South 105
Pan-Fried Cajun Butter Blackened Tofu 105
Simply Good Southern Mac and Cheese 106
Tossed Salad Greens with Avocado, Black Beans, and Fresh Coriander Vinaigrette 107
Family Kebab Night 109
Kofta Skewers 109
BBQ Tofu and Grilled Pineapple Skewers 110
Veggie and Sausage Kebabs 111
Chicken Pasta Bake with Simple Bag Salad and Dressing 113
Something to Comfort Your Soul 114
Slow Cooker Chick'n Noodle Soup 115
Warm Butter Biscuits 116
Garden Salad 117
Spaghetti Ragù and Market Bread 121
Chipotle Plant Beef and Bean Tostadas 123
Fresh Cilantro Pesto Pasta with Curry Tomato Salad and Pimiento Cheese Toast 125

Creole Tempeh with Wilted Collards and Jasmine Rice 127–28
Creamy Chipotle and Fresh Tomato Spaghetti with Grilled Zucchini and Roasted Yams 131
Sriracha Meatloaf with Steamed Rice and Sautéed Baby Bok Choy 133
BBQ Tofu Steaks with Wedged Roasted Yams 135
Macho Burritos 137
My American Guy Cheeseburger 139
Buffalo Portobello Burgers 141
Creole Sloppy Joe 143
Oyster Mushroom Po' Boys 145

Life's Little Joys 147

Pajamas and Pancakes Brunch Party! 150
Funfetti Pancakes 151
Mama's Golden Melon Milk 153
Good Morning Good-Belly Strawberry Smoothie 155
Sausage and Egg Breakfast Burrito 157
Yogurt Chia Pudding with Banana Bread and Breakfast Sausage 159
All-American Kiddo Lunch 161
Tame the Hunger Monster Grilled Cheese and Easy Tomato Soup 163
Papa's Black Beans and Veggie Rice with Sweet Plantains (Maduros) 165
Auntie's Tofu Chili Cornbread 167
Hidden Veggie Pasta with Nut-Butter Cracker Sandwiches 169
Blackened Tofu Burgers with Sliced Avocado and Strawberries 171
Black Pepper Chicken Fried Tofu with Cheesy Steamed Broccoli and Carrots 173
"Reel Fun Movie Playdate" 175
JUST Fried Egg and Cheese Sandwiches 177
Chick'n Noodle Soup Leftovers with Cornbread 179
Pan-Fried Adobo Tofu 181
Mama Made Pepperoni Pizza Pockets with Buttery Sweet Peas 183–84
Lunch Box Ginger Ramen with Scrambled Egg and Steamed Edamame 187
Chicken Burgers with Green Bean Fries 188
Shredded or Broken Tofu Tacos 190
Bacon Chicken Pasta Bake Leftovers with Garlic Bread 193
Baba's Smoked Tofu Cold Cuts Sammie 195
Auntie's Meaty Kid-Pleasin' Lasagna 196
Quesadillas and Tajín Butter Street Corn 199

The Sweetness of Life 201

Chocolate Chunk Fudgie Brownies 203
Auntie's Salted Chocolate Chip Cookies 205
My Sweet Georgia Peach 207
Vanilla Caramel Apple Sprinkle Ice-Cream Sammies 211
Strawberry Shortcake with Skillet Jam and Whipped Cream 213
Granny's Apple Crisp à la Mode 215
Box Banana Bread 217
Auntie's Secret Strawberry Box Bundt Cake with Lemon Cream Cheese Glaze 219
Fresh Blueberry Icebox Pie 221
Strawberry Shortcake Ice-Cream Bars 223

Metric Conversion Chart 225
With Gratitude 228
Index 233

Foreword by Stevie Wonder

Makini's cooking is filled with love and joy.

My music takes one on a journey of love, possibility, hope, and compassion. To get us there, I must be fed well. How I eat determines how I play, how I sing, how I'm able to interact and put out the power necessary to carry us on that voyage. When I am feeding off the land, eating a healthy plant-based diet, I'm also getting the food from the source of the soul, which comes from the energies that you're able to receive from the universe, you dig?

I describe Makini as compassionate. She is a wholesome woman. She is passionate about serving people in a healthy way and that means she has had to have compassion to understand the value of eating in the way that keeps you alive and sustains your life. Her care and her love in her cooking helped me on my *Songs in the Key of Life* tour because it ain't heavy how sometimes eating a meat-based diet can make you feel heavy. Makini's food made me feel full yet still light and fulfilled.

Being plant-based is a beautiful experience. I say beautiful, meaning that people who enjoy a diet that comes from the earth, that's from the source, from the earth. I believe in the earth and from the earth there are solutions to every problem that we know exists. The secret and the key are finding it. Makini's cooking will excite and satisfy you; you will become open to how much there is on the earth.

In this book you will learn more about the importance of eating healthily and you will come to know how to prepare good, satisfying plant-based meals. It's like the old saying, give a man a fish he will eat for a day; teach a man to fish and you feed him for a lifetime. With Makini's cooking, you get the information from an expert and know how to do it yourself forever and live a healthy lifestyle forever. Makini can teach you how to become vegan for the rest of your life if you desire. Her ways should be passed on from generation to generation, for generations to come.

When a person is able to put their soul in something like she does, you can feel it. With cooking, not only can you taste it, but you can feel it in the bread and body of the food, in the very way she prepares it. Makini does it with joy. When you have joy, when you do something like this, you'll see in your spirit. It makes the food feel happy . . . sort of delightful. Simple goodness.

—Stevie Wonder

Introduction: What Is Simple Goodness?

To me, simple goodness is the ease of making dinner with a few ingredients from the local bodega or from your garden. It's about using what you have. Simple goodness is about the foods your family loves and celebrates, from the pit BBQ your daddy cooked to your mom's Saturday morning breakfast.

For me, simply good food is home-cooked food. It's food filled with emotions, memories, and sentiment and it captures time perfectly. It's the taste of childhood: A hint of the aroma of cinnamon and spices remind me of the holiday season baking pies, cookies, and cakes with my mom. The smell of mesquite burning brings me right back to summertime in Alabama with my dad smoking tofu in a BBQ pit.

These simply good recipes are meals that are prepared and cooked with a focus on a familiar, thoughtful, and uncomplicated way of cooking. I use plant-based, high-quality ingredients and plain, straightforward cooking skills. One of my goals is to emphasize the ease of plant-based cooking by providing no-fuss recipes. Overall, *Simple Goodness* is about celebrating the natural flavors and textures of fresh, whole ingredients along with some of the leading plant-based brands on the market today and taking pleasure in the process of preparing and sharing meals with loved ones. What I hope to create with you is a powerful reminder of the warmth, love, and care that comes from sharing homemade dishes with the people we are most fond of.

When I opened my restaurant Plum Bistro in 2009, veganism was still relatively uncommon in the broader restaurant world. Over the past fifteen years, everyone, including many restaurants, seems to be trending more and more toward veganism every day, giving us an awesome opportunity to remake our lives and diets with plants. I love combining simple nutritious whole foods—such as grains, greens, legumes, fruits, nuts, and berries—with exciting new types of tofu and plant-based meats, milks, cheeses, and eggs. These recipes are intended to inspire you and enlighten you to the delicious possibilities of a familiar, sustainable, simply good plant-based life.

What you will find in this book is familiarity. I won't send you flying in all different directions for unique ingredients. In fact, I would be willing to guess you already have many if not most ingredients necessary to make these recipes in your pantry. And if not? You can go shopping at your local grocery store or your favorite big-box store. You'll use nationally available brands that are recognizable and simply good.

I've organized the recipe chapters in a way that's not surprising. We start with pantry essentials and some flavor basics (dips, seasonings, spreads), which you'll want to keep on hand. From there we go to quick weekday breakfasts and then more leisurely Saturday and Sunday morning brunch ideas, followed by lunches and lighter meals, full-course suppers, and a section just for kids. Finally, what would simple goodness be without a little sweetness in our life: we finish with desserts.

While every recipe here is special, the kids' section is extra special. One of the most important people in my life is my nephew Yaqeen. The Life's Little Joys section showcases easy, delicious, kid-focused meals that Yaqeen and I put together. If you're an auntie like me—or a mama, papa, nana, grandpop, or anyone who has kids in their life—you are going to love these recipes. These meals are great for lunch boxes or anytime your little one is hungry. There are also yummy nutrient-packed smoothies for breakfast and a delicious family meal for dinner that your little one can help you make.

Speaking of bigger meals, I have to tell you that Everyday Suppers is one of my favorite sections of the book. These recipes do for us longtime vegans and committed plant-based folks what has not been done before: they feed the revolution on a beautiful plate with a fork and knife. Supper doesn't have to be fancy, but it should be flavorful and satisfying. If you are a person who likes full meals planned out for you, you'll find them here. If you don't want to make the full meal, the individual recipes work great as stand-alones: just do what works for you. You can mix and match, whatever you like. I just know from working with and feeding people from all walks of life that, when it comes to vegan food, sometimes it's easiest to have meals mapped out for you. However you put your meals together, I hope they bring you joy.

I believe we have a chance to remake our world with what we choose to include in our diet, and we have the opportunity to choose love and change. Together, those things can move us forward toward a diet lighter in our bellies, gentler on our bodies, and kinder to the planet. I am so excited you decided to take this book home with you, and I hope it becomes the book you reach for when you're looking for something good to eat. I am looking forward to sharing what I have learned with you, and I really hope this book illuminates a path forward into a plant-based life—for you and all those you celebrate and, most importantly, love.

Herb Oil
Bacon Oil

Stocking Your Kitchen for a Plant-Based Life

Being a plant-based chef in the industry for nearly twenty years, I have tasted many vegan products, and I want to share my favorites with you. If you are new to veganism, you may not know where to start. If you have been vegan for many many years, I know you may be comfortable with your current way of doing things, but I encourage you to try this way at least once. Think of this list as curated especially for you by your own personal chef.

SIMPLY GOOD PANTRY ITEMS

Here's what I like to keep on hand. I've noted brands I like and that I use in my kitchen, which are available nationally. Remember, vegan products are not meat products, and there is a very wide range in tastes and flavors. You can certainly use whatever you have on hand but know that these recipes have been tested with these products.

COOK'S NOTE: Though Makini's is my brand for both mesquite tofu and chorizo taco mix, it may not have been tested in your region, so please try your favorite smoked tofu or tempeh brand as a mesquite replacement. You can also try your favorite plant-based chorizo or pastrami.

GOYA
Adobo
SMOKED PAPRIKA
CHICKEN SALT
VEGAN
RUMMO
LASAGNE Nº 83
WHEAT NOODLE
Natierra
ORGANIC BLUEBERRIES
Embasa
GOYA
Joy
SUGAR
TRADER JOE'S
Baking Soda
365
Organic Tomato Sauce
Campbell's
Tomato
SOUP
MUIR GLEN
ORGANIC
DICED
Kidney Beans
MUIR GLEN
Pinto Beans
RAO'S
HOMEMADE
MARINARA
Tomato Paste
Gochujang
SANTA CRUZ
organic
HEINZ
TOMATO KETCHUP
SANTA CRUZ
organic
Hunt's
Great Northern Beans
GOYA
EDEN
ORGANIC
GARBANZO BEANS
BOOM CHICKA POP
Annie's
Peel-A-Parts
DELICIOUS CRUNCH
VEGAN
DANDIES

PLANT-BASED PROTEIN

PLANT BEEF AND PORK

Before the Butcher Uncut Burger Ground
Beyond Burger
Beyond Sausage, Hot Italian
Beyond Steak
Impossible Beef (ground)
Impossible Sausage, savory
Impossible Sausage, spicy
Impossible Wild Nuggies
MorningStar Farms Sausage Patties
Trader Joe's Plant-Based Pepperoni Slices

PLANT CHICKEN

Daring Original Plant Chicken Pieces
Impossible Chicken Nuggets
MorningStar Farms Original Chik'n Patties
Rebellyous Plant-Based Nuggets

PLANT MEATS, OTHER

Gardein F'sh Filets
MorningStar Farms Corn Dogs

SEITAN

Blackbird Original Seitan
Franklin Farms
Makini's Chick'n Seitan
Makini's Naked Seitan

TEMPEH

LightLife
Turtle Island

TOFU

Hodo Soy, extra-firm and firm
House Foods, extra-firm and firm
Makini's Tofu (Baba's Smoked Tofu, Chorizo Taco Mix, Tofustrami [Pastrami])
Trader Joe's Organic Tofu (hot-pink label)

PLANT-BASED DAIRY ALTERNATIVES

BUTTER

Country Crock Plant Butter
Earth Balance
Flora Plant Butter
Violife Plant Butter

CHEESES

Daiya Cheddar & Mozza Shreds
Daiya Cheddar Slices
Follow Your Heart Dairy-Free Cheddar Shredded
Follow Your Heart Dairy-Free Cheese Parmesan
Follow Your Heart Dairy-Free Mozzarella Shredded
Go Veggie Grated Parmesan Style Topping
Violife dairy-free cheeses (sliced Cheddar, mature Cheddar, smoked provolone; shredded Colby Jack, mozzarella, Cheddar; shaved Parmesan)

Original
Crescent Dough Sheet
PLAIN
Silk
daiya
deliciously dairy-free
Forager
Best Foods
CHILI CRUNCH
unsweetened
SO DELICIOUS
ORGANIC
Annie's
Great Buttery Taste
IMPOSSIBLE
IMPOSSIBLE SAUSAGE MADE FROM PLANTS
TOFU
FOLLOW YOUR HEART
DAIRY-FREE CHEESE
Parmesan
Violife
ORIGINAL CREAM CHEESE
BEYOND BURGER
PLANT-BASED PATTIES
35% LESS SATURATED FAT
hodo
ORGANIC EXTRA FIRM TOFU
FETA

ICE CREAM

Oatly! Vanilla Non-dairy Frozen Dessert
Wicked Kitchen Vanilla

MILK, HEAVY CREAM, AND WHIPPING CREAM

Chobani Oatmilk Extra Creamy
Country Crock Plant Cream Heavy Whipping Cream Alternative
Edensoy Unsweetened Organic Soymilk
Flora Dairy-Free Multipurpose Crème
Silk Dairy-Free Heavy Whipping Cream Alternative
Silk Unsweet Organic Soy
Truwhip
Westsoy Organic Unsweetened Plain Soymilk

SOUR CREAM, YOGURT, AND CREAM CHEESE

Follow Your Heart Sour Cream
Forager Cashewmilk Yogurt
Silk soymilk yogurt
SO Delicious Unsweetened Coconutmilk Yogurt Alternative
Tofutti Cream Cheese
Violife Just Like Cream Cheese Original

MISCELLANEOUS PANTRY ITEMS

BREADING

Black Pepper Breading (page 16)
Panko Breading (page 17)

BROTH AND STOCK

Dragonfly Instant Artificial Chicken Flavor Broth
Veggie or vegan chicken stock (page 27)

CONDIMENTS, SAUCES, AND DRESSINGS

Best Foods Vegan Dressing & Spread
Bread and butter pickles
Coconut cream (Good & Gather Organic Unsweetened Coconut Cream, Kara Natural Coconut Cream, O Organics Coconut Cream, Thai Kitchen Unsweetened Coconut Cream)
Gochujang Fermented Hot Chile Paste
Hot pickled onions (see page 25 for a homemade version)
Soy sauce and tamari (San-J, Kikkoman)
Stubbs Mesquite Liquid Smoke
Stubbs Original Bar-B-Q Sauce
The Wizard's Organic Vegan Worcestershire Sauce

EGG REPLACEMENTS

Applesauce
Chia and flax seeds, to make homemade chia and flax "eggs"
Ener-G Egg Replacer
JUST Egg

FREEZE-DRIED FRUIT

Trader Joe's Freeze Dried Blueberries
Trader Joe's Freeze Dried Strawberries

tofu
EXTRA FIRM
CHICKEN NUGGETS
MADE FROM PLANTS
13g PROTEIN PER SERVING
60% LESS SATURATED FAT
NET WT. 13.5oz (383g)
CONTAINS NO ANIMAL PRODUCTS
WOW NO COW!
THE ORIGINAL
1 pint (473 ml)
100% Vegan
BEN & JERRY'S
nondairy
Mint Chocolate Cookie
plant-based
lightly seasoned
chick'n
NON GMO Project VERIFIED
Puff Pastry SHEETS
PEPPERIDGE FARM
Amy's PIZZA
VEGAN MARGHERITA
MADE WITH ORGANIC VEGAN CHEEZE, TOMATOES & BASIL
salted caramel
CASHEWMILK

100% PLANT CHICKEN
CHICKEN NUGGETS MADE
VEGGIE
CRISPY OUTSIDE. JUICY INSIDE.
rebellyous foods
NO HARM. NO FOWL.
PLANT-BASED TENDERS
SERVING SUGGESTION
NET WT 7.8 OZ (221g)
KEEP FROZEN
COCONUTMILK
SO DELICIOUS
DAIRY FREE
SHREDDED
IMPOSSIBLE
IMPOSSIBLE SAUSAGE MADE FROM PLANTS
KITCHEN
VANILLA
100% PLANT BASED
Baba's Smoked Tofu

ORIGINAL CHIK PATTIES
BEYOND MEAT
BEYOND BURGER
PLANT-BASED PATTIES

KALE
MADE GOOD
What makes this product MadeGood?
Violife
100% Vegan
just like
365
WHOLE FOODS MARKET
Pinto Beans
FOLLOW YOUR HEART
DAIRY-FREE CHEESE
Parmesan

Simply Good Flavor Staples

Sometimes all it takes is a simple dip or sauce or a zippy spicy condiment to make a boring meal special. These are items I like to make ahead and have in the fridge. If you take the time to prepare these flavor staples, your cooking journey will be that much easier.

Dips That Double as Sauces

Are you tired of being the vegan who never gets the creamy dip with your veggies or the yummy sauce with your sandwich? Well, move over hummus. These tasty creamy dips that double as sauces are a vegan's dream addition to any veggie tray. They keep in the fridge for three to five days, and they will brighten up your sandwiches too.

Jalapeño Dip

MAKES 2 CUPS

Cilantro plus jalapeño plus mayo equals a zingy, fresh dip for veggies or chips. Or slather it on your favorite burger.

2 cups vegan mayonnaise
¼ cup chopped cilantro (stems are fine)
2 tablespoons freshly squeezed lime juice
1 large jalapeño pepper with seeds, chopped
2 teaspoons sea salt
½ teaspoon chopped fresh garlic (optional)

1. In a blender, bullet, or food processor, place the mayo, cilantro, lime juice, jalapeño, salt, and garlic, if using. Pulse until the ingredients are combined. You can also combine by hand: simply mince the cilantro, jalapeño, and garlic, if using, and mix with all the other ingredients in a small bowl. This will keep in the fridge for 3–5 days.

Dill Dip

MAKES 2 CUPS

I love this as an all-purpose veggie dip, but it's especially good with fries. Hey, potatoes are vegetables too!

2 cups vegan mayonnaise
2 tablespoons fresh dill
1 tablespoon roasted garlic
1 tablespoon freshly squeezed lemon juice
1 teaspoon sea salt
½ teaspoon freshly ground black pepper

1. In a blender, bullet, or food processor, place the mayo, dill, roasted garlic, lemon juice, salt, and pepper. Pulse until the ingredients are combined. You can also combine by hand: simply mince the dill and garlic and mix with all the other ingredients in a small bowl. This will keep in the fridge for 3–5 days.

Chipotle Dip

MAKES 2 CUPS

Add a touch of heat to your veggies or french-fry tray with this smoky dip. It's great on tacos and burritos too. Note: You can find chipotle peppers in adobo sauce in most grocery stores in the Mexican or Latin food aisle. They can be spicy, so start small and adjust as needed. They'll last in the fridge for up to a week or so.

2 cups vegan mayonnaise
¼ cup chopped chipotle peppers in adobo sauce
1 tablespoon freshly squeezed lime juice
2 teaspoons cilantro
1½ teaspoons sea salt
½ teaspoon chopped fresh garlic (optional)

1. In a blender, bullet, or food processor, place the mayo, chipotle peppers, lime juice, cilantro, salt, and garlic, if using. Pulse until the ingredients are combined. You can also combine by hand: simply mince the chipotles, cilantro, and garlic, if using, and mix with all the other ingredients in a small bowl. This will keep in the fridge for 3–5 days.

Papa's Sammie Sauce

MAKES 2 CUPS

Nothing beats a good sandwich, and sauce is key. If you are a grill king like my dad was, spread this on some bread and throw whatever you grilled on top of it. This is my go-to, all-purpose sandwich sauce. It's mild and super flavorful, great for the entire tribe, for everyone from eight years old to eighty.

2 cups vegan mayonnaise
¼ cup minced fresh parsley
2 tablespoons freshly squeezed lemon juice
¼ cup plain, unsweetened plant milk
1 teaspoon chopped fresh garlic
1 teaspoon sea salt
¼ teaspoon freshly ground black pepper

1. In a blender, place the mayo, parsley, lemon juice, plant milk, garlic, sea salt, and black pepper. Blend until the sauce turns a fun green color. You can also combine by hand: just add all the ingredients to a bowl and mix well. This will keep in the fridge for 3–5 days.

Tabasco Aioli

MAKES ABOUT 1 CUP

As you may be able to tell by now, I love a good sammie or dipping sauce, and this one is equally high on my go-to list. I use it on my Oyster Mushroom Po' Boys (page 145), but you can add this to your rotation anytime you need to add a spicy kick to your sandwich or dip for veggies.

1 cup vegan mayonnaise
¼ teaspoon onion powder
¼ teaspoon garlic powder
½ teaspoon smoked paprika
Sea salt
As many shots of Tabasco as you can handle

1. In a small mixing bowl, mix the mayo with the onion powder, garlic powder, smoked paprika, salt, and shots of Tabasco. Stir all the ingredients until well combined. Store in the fridge for up to a week.

Tajín Butter

MAKES ABOUT 1½ CUPS

This butter really delivers on flavor. I like to use this on cornbread or grilled corn. I've even tried it on some regular ole toast with a grilled veggie sandwich. The flavor will not disappoint.

½ cup (1 stick) plant butter
¼ cup vegan mayonnaise (I like Best Foods)
1 tablespoon Tajín Mexican chili
½ cup grated vegan Parmesan cheese
1 tablespoon or more chopped fresh cilantro
1 teaspoon Cajun seasoning
½ teaspoon minced fresh garlic
1 teaspoon sea salt

1. Remove the butter from the fridge and allow it to come to room temperature. In a medium bowl, mix the butter, mayo, Tajín, Parmesan, cilantro, Cajun seasoning, garlic, and salt. Store in the fridge in a small tub or jar; it will keep for about a week.

Yogurt Tahini Sauce

MAKES 1 CUP

The type of yogurt is key here: don't go substituting just any ole yogurt now. This brand of unsweetened coconut yogurt has a tangy, slightly sour taste that is close to Greek yogurt. It's not exact, as it is a bit thinner, but a good second. If coconut yogurt is not your thing, try using Best Foods vegan mayo. It will be a bit richer. I love using this on anything Mediterranean inspired or even on a salad. It's so nice to have sauces like these to complete the eating experience.

¾ cup SO Delicious Unsweetened Coconutmilk Yogurt Alternative
¼ cup minced yellow onion
2 tablespoons tahini
2 tablespoons freshly squeezed lemon juice
1½ tablespoons olive oil
1 tablespoon chopped fresh cilantro
1 tablespoon chopped fresh mint
1½ tablespoons chopped fresh garlic
1½ teaspoons sea salt

1. In a small bowl, place the yogurt, onion, tahin, lemon juice, olive oil, cilantro, mint, garlic, and salt. Mix all the ingredients until well combined. Store in the fridge in a mason jar; it will keep for 3–5 days.

Fresh Cilantro Pesto

MAKES ABOUT 5 CUPS

I love traditional pesto, but I also love to shake things up. I use almonds here instead of pine nuts. The secret ingredients are mint and cilantro, which make a bright, fresh flavor. The citrus and jalapeño add a little kick that's great on pasta, sandwiches, and roasted veggies. Or just spread it on some bread and add some sliced avocado and salt for a yummy snack.

4 cups packed chopped fresh cilantro
¼ cup chopped mint
1 tablespoon chopped jalapeño pepper
2 teaspoons chopped fresh garlic
1½ cups olive oil
2 tablespoons almonds
4 tablespoons freshly squeezed lemon juice
½ cup grated vegan Parmesan cheese

1. In a blender, place the cilantro, mint, jalapeño, garlic, olive oil, almonds, lemon juice, and cheese; blend to a smooth pesto consistency. Store in a mason jar in the fridge; it will keep for a good week or so.

Black Pepper Breading

MAKES 4 CUPS

I love to have a good all-purpose breading on hand at all times. If you're anything like me, sometimes you want to fry or air-fry something, but you don't want to make breading every time. This one is peppery and robust. Use it in recipes like Calamari Lettuce Wraps (page 71), Eggplant Parmesan with Alfredo Rigatoni (page 103), and Buffalo Portobello Burgers (page 141).

4 cups all-purpose flour
½ cup freshly ground black pepper
3 teaspoons sea salt
¼ cup onion powder
¼ cup garlic powder

1. In a mixing bowl, place the flour, black pepper, salt, onion powder, and garlic powder and mix until well combined. Store in an airtight container; it will keep for about 2 weeks.

Mild Black Pepper Breading

MAKES 2 CUPS

If you are feeding little ones or folks who don't love a lot of kick, this breading is modified for those palates. This is half the quantity of the Black Pepper Breading: go ahead and double the recipe if you want to keep more on hand.

2 cups all-purpose flour
2 teaspoons freshly ground black pepper
1½ teaspoons sea salt
2 tablespoons onion powder
2 tablespoons garlic powder

1. In a mixing bowl, place the flour, black pepper, salt, onion powder, and garlic powder and mix until well combined. Store in an airtight container; it will keep for 2 weeks.

Panko Breading

MAKES ABOUT 4 CUPS

I like using panko as a breading from time to time because these nice flaky breadcrumbs don't pack together when coating food, so your food stays crispier longer. Panko is just right for things like portobellos, or if you want a crispy topping for your mac and cheese.

4 cups panko breadcrumbs
2 tablespoons sea salt
¼ cup dried oregano leaves
1 tablespoon freshly ground black pepper
2 tablespoons paprika

1. In a mixing bowl, place the panko, salt, dried oregano leaves, black pepper, and paprika. Mix until well combined. This can be made ahead and stored in an airtight container for a few weeks in a cool, dry cupboard.

Taco Seasoning

MAKES ABOUT ¼ CUP

Remember that time you wanted to make a Mexican dish and you realized you'd already used your last packet of seasoning last Taco Tuesday? Make this seasoning in advance and feel free to size it up: you can have tacos every day of the week. Use this seasoning in recipes such as refried beans. Kept in a seasoning shaker, you can even use it on corn chips to spice them up a bit.

1 tablespoon chili powder
2 teaspoons onion powder
1 teaspoon garlic powder
1 teaspoon paprika
1 teaspoon dried oregano leaves
1 teaspoon ground cumin
¼ teaspoon sea salt

1. In a small mixing bowl, place the chili powder, onion powder, garlic powder, paprika, dried oregano leaves, cumin, and salt and mix until well combined. Store in an airtight container; it will keep for a few weeks.

Vegan Ranch

MAKES ABOUT 2½ CUPS

This plant twist on a classic really hits the spot.

- 2 cups vegan mayonnaise (I like Best Foods or use your favorite brand)
- 2 tablespoons plain, unsweetened plant milk (I like soy)
- 2 tablespoons vinegar
- 1 teaspoon Dijon mustard
- 2 tablespoons minced fresh parsley
- 1 tablespoon sea salt
- 1 teaspoon freshly ground black pepper

1. In a small mixing bowl, place the mayo, plant milk, vinegar, Dijon mustard, parsley, salt, and pepper. Mix until well combined. Store in the fridge for a week or so.

COOK'S NOTE: If your mayo is a bit thick, use ¼ cup of plant milk to thin it out if needed. If your mayo is on the thinner side (like Best Foods), use 2 tablespoons of milk to thin it out if you like.

Buffalo Sauce

MAKES ABOUT 2 CUPS

I am so glad buffalo sauce is vegan! It's one of those classic flavors that many of us really enjoy. I love dipping my french fries or fried cauliflower florets in it or spreading it on a Buffalo Portobello Burger (page 141).

- 4 cups Frank's RedHot Buffalo Wings sauce
- ½ cup (1 stick) mild-flavored plant butter (I like Country Crock or Earth Balance)
- ¼ cup natural cane sugar
- 2 tablespoons fresh minced garlic

1. In a medium saucepan, place the hot sauce, butter, sugar, and garlic. Over medium-high heat, bring the sauce to a simmer and cook for 10 minutes to combine flavors. Chill and store in an airtight container for a week or more in the fridge.

Sweet Chili Sauce

MAKES ABOUT 3 CUPS

This is a great condiment. I use it as a dipping sauce for my mushroom calamari, but you can use it on whatever you like. It's great for spring rolls or fresh rolls too.

3 cups of sweet chili sauce (I like Mae Ploy)
2 tablespoons peeled and chopped fresh ginger
1 tablespoon lime zest
1½ tablespoons freshly squeezed lime juice
1 tablespoon tamari
2 tablespoons chopped fresh mint leaves
2 tablespoons chopped fresh cilantro

1. In a small saucepot, place the chili sauce, ginger, lime zest, lime juice, and tamari. Bring to a boil and cook for 2–3 minutes. Turn the heat off and allow sauce to cool completely, then add the herbs. Store in the fridge for 7–10 days.

COOK'S NOTE: Adding the fresh herbs once the sauce is completely cool keeps it from becoming bitter, so don't skip this step.

Marinara Sauce

MAKES 8–9 CUPS

I love keeping a batch of red sauce in my freezer or fridge. Having this on hand makes mealtime super quick: heat up some sauce, add your pasta and whatever quick veggie you have in the fridge on the side, and you've got an easy, delicious dinner. Or grab a bag of pizza dough and a bag of your favorite shredded vegan cheese for homemade cheese pizza and call it good.

¼ cup olive oil
½ cup diced yellow onion
1 teaspoon chopped fresh garlic
½ cup red wine
1 (32-ounce) can tomato sauce
1 (32-ounce) can whole tomatoes
¼ cup chopped fresh parsley
¼ cup chopped fresh basil
2 tablespoons natural cane sugar
1 teaspoon sea salt
½ teaspoon freshly ground black pepper
1 teaspoon dried oregano leaves
Generous pinch of chili flakes
2 tablespoons plant butter (Country Crock or your favorite nondairy butter)

1. Place the olive oil in a soup pot and heat to medium high. Add the onion and garlic; cook for 3 to 4 minutes, or until the onion is translucent. Add the red wine. Allow the wine to cook for about 3 minutes until the alcohol cooks off, then add the tomato sauce and whole tomatoes, parsley, basil, sugar, salt, black pepper, oregano, and chili flakes. Cook for 25–30 minutes. Turn off the heat and add the butter; allow it to melt and then mix it in. For a smooth marinara, blend all the ingredients in batches. This will keep in the fridge for 3–4 days or in the freezer for 3 months.

Fresh Herb Oil

MAKES 2 CUPS

I was on the road with Stevie Wonder, and we were in North Carolina. Thus far I had been working in kitchens full of male chefs and large male energy, and then I met a rad female chef who had a big team of mostly guys, and she ran a tight ship. We chatted a lot about being women in such a hugely male-dominated industry and how our unique female perspective offers something different. She gave me this recipe and told me to use it on everything, and I do use it on everything. To start, try it on Citrus Black-Eyed Pea Salad (page 67), drizzle it on roasted sweet potatoes, or use it as a dip for bread.

2 cups olive oil blend
1 shallot, minced
1 tablespoon minced garlic
½ cup chopped fresh parsley
¼ cup fresh thyme leaves, pulled from stem
½ cup chopped fresh oregano

1. In a small bowl, place the olive oil, shallot, garlic, and the herbs—parsley, thyme, and oregano—and mix all the ingredients. Store in the fridge in an airtight container; it will last for a good week or more.

Sun-Dried Tomato Sammie Relish

MAKES ABOUT ½ CUP

This relish is truly versatile—there are no limits to how you can use it. The sun-dried tomatoes give it a nice, sweet tang. Try it on everything from sammies to baked potatoes and grilled veggies, or just spread it on some good bread.

¼ cup chopped sun-dried tomatoes packed in oil, minced
3 tablespoons minced onion
1 teaspoon chopped fresh garlic
½ cup chopped fresh parsley or cilantro
1 tablespoon chopped jalapeño pepper
½ cup avocado oil
½ teaspoon sea salt
2 generous pinches freshly ground black pepper

1. In a small mixing bowl, place the sun-dried tomatoes, onion, garlic, parsley, jalapeño, avocado oil, salt, and pepper and mix well to combine. Store in a mason jar; it will keep for a week to 10 days in the pantry.

Bacon Bits and Bacon Oil

MAKES 2 CUPS

If you are new to plant-based eating and miss the smoky flavor of bacon, you will miss it no longer. This two-fer recipe gives you both the most flavorful bacon bits you can use as a topping, as well as bacony oil you can use in dressings, on eggs, or as a drizzle on salads, soups, and pastas. If you want to make a smoky-flavored butter, add it to your favorite plant-based version.

2 cups Baba's Mesquite Smoked Tofu, minced, or LightLife Tempeh Smoky Bacon, crumbled (it will not be as crispy-crunchy, though)
2 cups avocado oil

1. Cut the tofu into cubes and place in a food processor. Pulse until minced into random-size pieces, about the size of bacon bits; make sure not to grind the cubes to a paste.
2. Place the avocado oil in a medium pot and bring to medium heat. Add the tofu and cook for 3 minutes, until starting to crisp. Remove from the heat right before the tofu gets too crispy: it will continue to cook once removed from heat, and it's very easy to burn. If you want your bits to be a bit softer, cook for 2 minutes.
3. If you are using tempeh, crumble the tempeh by hand into pea-size pieces and pan-fry in oil on medium heat. LightLife won't crisp the same way as Baba's, but it will turn golden and fragrant.
4. Once cooled, store the bits in a mason jar. Use them and the bacon oil together or separately: use the bits as an ingredient in various dishes, and use the oil to add extra flavor to everything from eggs to salad dressing.

Bacon Vinaigrette

MAKES ABOUT 1 CUP

Want to make simple greens pop with an exciting burst of flavor? This vinaigrette uses the Bacon Bits and Bacon Oil recipe for smoky goodness. The tangy pops of stone-ground mustard dance on your taste buds, and the fresh garlic grounds the vinaigrette with solid flavorfulness. Keep this one on hand in the fridge; I guarantee you will up your salad game.

6 tablespoons bacon bits (page 21)
½ cup bacon oil (page 21)
2 tablespoons stone-ground mustard
2 tablespoons agave
2 tablespoons cider or red wine vinegar
2 teaspoons chopped fresh garlic
1 tablespoon chopped fresh parsley
½ teaspoon sea salt
½ teaspoon pepper

1. In a small mixing bowl, place the bacon bits and oil, mustard, agave, vinegar, garlic, parsley, salt, and pepper and mix well to combine. Store in a mason jar; it will keep for a good week or so.

Burger Seasoning

MAKES ABOUT 2 CUPS

Keep this seasoning on hand anytime you want to give your plant-based meats a little extra zing. You can also dust it on fries.

¼ cup paprika
¾ cup dried parsley flakes
2 tablespoons garlic powder
1 tablespoon onion powder
¼ cup kosher salt
¼ cup freshly ground black pepper
1–2 tablespoons cayenne pepper or more, if you like it spicy

1. In a mixing bowl, place the paprika, dried parsley, garlic powder, onion powder, salt, black pepper, and cayenne pepper. Mix all the ingredients until well combined. Store in an airtight container; it will keep for a few weeks in a cool, dry place.

Sautéed Onions

MAKES ABOUT 2 CUPS

This is a simple, straightforward condiment. One recipe should work for four burgers, but if you want more, go ahead and double the recipe.

1 large yellow onion
2–3 tablespoons cooking oil (avocado, safflower, or canola)
½ teaspoon sea salt

1. Slice the onion into ¼-inch rings. In a large sauté pan or skillet, heat the oil over medium-high heat. Add the onions and cook, stirring frequently, until they are soft and golden-brown, for 8–10 minutes. These onions are best made fresh but can be cooked ahead and stored in the refrigerator; simply reheat when ready to use.

Special Sauce

MAKES ABOUT 2 CUPS

You know this sauce—it's got that zing that makes a certain fast-food burger its own thing. Now we vegans can have it too! Slather it all over your burgers or any sandwich. This recipe makes about 2 cups; use it anytime you want that special flavor.

1 cup vegan mayonnaise (I like Best Foods)
2 tablespoons yellow mustard
¼ cup sweet relish
¼ cup ketchup
¼ cup BBQ sauce (your favorite kind)

1. In a mixing bowl, place the mayo, yellow mustard, sweet relish, ketchup, and BBQ sauce. Mix all the ingredients until well combined. The sauce can be stored in a jar in the fridge for a week or so.

Wedged Roasted Yams

MAKES 3 SERVINGS

1½–2 pounds white-flesh yams (1–2, depending on size)
¼ cup Fresh Herb Oil (page 20) or olive or avocado oil
½ teaspoon sea salt
¼ teaspoon pepper
2 tablespoons grated vegan Parmesan cheese, divided
2 teaspoons chopped fresh garlic
Fresh cilantro, for garnish
Green onion, sliced, for garnish

1. Preheat the oven to 350–400°F.
2. Cut the yams in half crosswise. If your yams are really large, cut them lengthwise in half and into about ¾-inch wedges or 4–6 wedges per half. Smaller yams will yield 3–4 wedges per half.
3. Place the wedges in a bowl and toss with the herb oil, salt, pepper, Parmesan, and garlic until well coated.
4. Lay the wedges cut-side down on a baking sheet. Cook covered in foil for 20 minutes and then uncovered for 15 minutes. Garnish with cilantro and onion before serving.

Spanish Rice

MAKES 4 CUPS

The spices here add a zingy flavor boost to your basic rice. This rice is great with all things Mexican-food inspired.

2 tablespoons vegetable oil
2 cups long-grain rice
1 teaspoon minced garlic
2 tablespoons minced onion
4 cups water or veggie stock
8 ounces tomato juice
1 teaspoon sea salt
6 stems cilantro (optional)

1. Heat oil in a large frying pan on medium heat. Add the rice and cook, stirring constantly to ensure it does not burn. The rice will start to turn golden-brown in 3–5 minutes.
2. When the rice is golden-brown, add the garlic and onion and give them a stir, then add the water, tomato juice, and salt. Stir the rice and add the cilantro, if using. Cover the pan. Let simmer for 30–40 minutes, or until cooked and no liquid is left. Fluff before serving and enjoy.

Pico de Gallo

MAKES 4 CUPS

I have been using this recipe in the restaurant for well over a decade. It's a great basic salsa to have on hand. But it's not just your regular pico de gallo: the jalapeño brings the heat and my secret ingredient, orange, adds a fun burst of flavor to this traditional condiment. Serve it with chips and guac, on sandwiches, or on JUST Eggs. I use it in my Macho Burritos and breakfast tacos (recipes page 137 and 53–54, respectively).

4 cups diced Roma tomatoes, cut into ¼-inch pieces
½ cup diced yellow onion, cut into ¼-inch pieces
½ cup peeled, seeded, and diced orange
½ cup chopped fresh cilantro
¼ cup minced jalapeño pepper
¼ cup freshly squeezed lemon juice, or juice of 1 lemon
2 teaspoons sea salt
½ teaspoon freshly ground black pepper

1. In a bowl, place the tomatoes, onion, orange, cilantro, jalapeño, lemon juice, salt, and black pepper. Mix until well combined. Store in a mason jar in the fridge; it will last a couple of days.

Pepper Pot Pickled Onions

MAKES ABOUT 1½ CUPS

My dad would try to pickle *anything*! I guess that was the southerner in him. He also had some pretty wise habits: he would always yell at us, "Don't stick your fingers in the pickle jar! The pickles will go bad!" I always remember these gems and love sharing his experience and knowledge of working with food. This peppery, spicy condiment can be used on anything you feel needs a little extra heat.

1 medium red onion, julienned
3–5 habañero peppers, thinly sliced
1 cup freshly squeezed lemon juice, or juice of 4 lemons
2 tablespoons cider vinegar
1 tablespoon dried oregano leaves
1 teaspoon sea salt
½ teaspoon freshly ground black pepper
2 cloves garlic, smashed

1. In a pickling jar or a container with a lid, place the onion, habañero peppers, lemon juice, vinegar, and oregano leaves. Season with salt and pepper, and add the garlic. Seal the jar or container and shake, shake, shake it, baby, to combine. Store for 4–6 hours to let the heat from the pepper release and the citrus pickle the onions. These pickled onions will keep in the fridge for 5–7 days.

Red Cabbage Lime Slaw

MAKES ABOUT 6 CUPS

This tasty slaw adds a zingy kick to whatever you are having. I use it on my fried chicken burger (page 188), but you can use it in a salad or your favorite wrap for a little added pizzazz.

1 bag coleslaw mix (toss the dressing or save it for later), or about 6 cups of shredded purple and green cabbage
½ cup sliced onion
½ cup chopped fresh cilantro
¼ cup sliced green onion
1 small jalapeño pepper, stemmed and julienned (to reduce heat, scrape out the seeds)
1 tablespoon sea salt and pepper, mixed
½ cup freshly squeezed lime juice
2 tablespoons natural cane sugar
¼ cup red wine vinegar
¼ cup avocado oil

1. In a large salad bowl, place the cabbage, onion, cilantro, green onion, jalapeño, salt and pepper, lime juice, sugar, red wine vinegar, and avocado oil. Toss all the ingredients together and allow to set for 4–6 hours or overnight.

Fresh Coriander Vinaigrette

MAKES ABOUT 1 CUP

Add this vinaigrette to your salad rotation for a tangy flavor burst.

1 tablespoon crushed coriander seeds
¼ cup white wine vinegar
¼ cup minced white onion
2 teaspoons minced fresh garlic
¼ cup chopped fresh cilantro
¾ cup olive oil blend
1½ teaspoons sea salt
½ teaspoon freshly ground black pepper

1. Combine the coriander seeds, vinegar, onion, garlic, cilantro, oil, salt, and pepper in a mason jar and shake, shake, shake it, baby, till well combined. Store in the fridge; it will keep for 5–7 days.

Veggie or Vegan Chicken Stock

MAKES ABOUT 2 QUARTS

Finding a good stock is the bane of any vegan's existence! Packaged stock is never quite as appealing as I would like it to be, so let's make our own. It's not difficult, and the flavor payoff is well worth it. The oil in this recipe is a game changer. This is great with just veggies, but if you are into a little extra flavor, add vegan chicken broth. Whatever you do, do you—and you will really enjoy using this as an ingredient.

½ cup avocado oil
½ large onion or 1 small onion, cut into quarters
2 large carrots, cut in half
3–4 ribs of celery, cut in half
¼ cup dry porcini mushrooms
¼ cup whole garlic or 8–10 cloves
1 tablespoon black peppercorns
8 sprigs thyme
12 stems fresh parsley
16 cups water
¼ cup vegan chicken broth (optional)

1. In a stockpot, place the avocado oil, onion, carrots, celery, porcini mushrooms, garlic, peppercorns, thyme, and parsley. Sauté on medium heat until the veggies start to turn golden-brown and become fragrant, for 4–6 minutes; be careful not to burn them. Add the water, cover, and cook for 45 minutes. Add the broth, if using. Allow to cool and pass through a strainer, pressing all the juice from the veggies. Stored in the fridge, it will last about a week or so; freeze for up to 3 months.

Gyro Spice Blend

MAKES 1 CUP

Sometimes I want a flavor kick that is a little bit savory, a little bit sweet, and all delicious. This Greek-inspired spice blend will add just the right amount of flavor to your favorite mushrooms. A little bit goes a long way!

2 tablespoons chopped fresh mint
2 tablespoons dried oregano leaves
1 tablespoon cinnamon
2 teaspoons freshly ground black pepper
1 teaspoon nutmeg
1 teaspoon sea salt
2 tablespoons ground coriander
2 tablespoons smoked paprika
2 teaspoons natural cane sugar
2 teaspoons garlic powder
2 tablespoons dried parsley flakes

1. Spread the mint out on a small pan or baking sheet and let it air-dry.
2. In a small mixing bowl, combine the oregano, cinnamon, black pepper, nutmeg, salt, coriander, paprika, sugar, garlic powder, and parsley flakes; stir in the mint once it is dry. Store in an airtight container. If your mint is not completely dry when you add it, store the mixture in the fridge. This dry spice mixture will keep for a few weeks.

Parmesan Herb Croutons

MAKES ABOUT 4 CUPS

Whenever I made croutons, I used to carefully cut the bread into evenly sized chunks. All that changed when I was having dinner at a neighbor's house. She served these yummy homemade croutons. Turns out her secret is to tear the bread to get those little crispy crunchies. So tear the bread for the tastiest croutons!

- 4 cups bread, torn into bite-size pieces (partially baked or stale bread works great)
- 2 tablespoons bacon oil (page 21) or avocado oil
- ¼ teaspoon or less sea salt
- 1–2 pinches freshly ground black pepper
- ¼ teaspoon fresh garlic or granulated garlic powder
- ½ teaspoon Italian seasoning
- 2 tablespoons grated vegan Parmesan cheese

1. Preheat the oven to 400°F.
2. Place the bread in a medium bowl. Add the bacon oil, salt, black pepper, garlic, Italian seasoning, and Parmesan. Toss all the ingredients until combined and transfer to a cookie sheet. Bake for 10 minutes or until crispy. Stored in a tight container, these croutons will keep for 3–5 days.

Strawberry Skillet Jam

MAKES ABOUT 4 CUPS

Summertime in Seattle means strawberries. We go strawberry picking, and before you know it, our house is overrun with strawberries. This quick skillet recipe makes great use of extra fruit without too much extra fuss. I use this jam with Strawberry Shortcake Ice-Cream Bars (page 223) or on biscuits or toast. You can even put this on top of some ice cream!

- 32-ounce container strawberries, roughly chopped, or about 6 cups
- 2 teaspoons lemon zest, or zest of 1 lemon
- ½ cup freshly squeezed lemon juice, or juice of 2 lemons
- ¾–1 cup natural cane sugar
- Generous pinch of sea salt

1. In a deep pan or saucepot, place the strawberries, lemon zest, lemon juice, sugar, and salt. On medium heat, cook the fruit for 30–40 minutes, or until it becomes thick like jam, keeping in mind it will thicken up more when cold. Remove from the heat and store in glass jars. The jam will keep about a week or so in the fridge.

Box Cornbread/Muffins

MAKES 12 MUFFINS

My father, a true old southerner, had some opinions about things like cornbread. He said sweet cornbread was a disgrace, but I secretly love the stuff. This recipe can be as sweet as you like or as sweet as the mix you use. I use Trader Joe's, but you can swap in any brand. I like to serve this with my Citrus Black-Eyed Pea Salad (page 67)—or just eat it hot from the pan!

- 1 box cornbread mix (I like Trader Joe's)
- ½ cup vegetable oil
- ¾ cup plain, unsweetened plant milk
- 3 tablespoons JUST Egg (optional)

1. Follow the cooking instructions on the box, using the oil and plant milk. Guess what: this cornbread does not need the JUST Egg. You can omit it altogether if you like, and the cornbread will be JUST fine.

Pimiento Cheese

MAKES ABOUT 4 CUPS

This is one of those throwback recipes that has so many origin stories. Wherever it came from, it usually has cheese, mayo, and pimientos and so is generally not available to vegans. Well, that's not true anymore. This cheesy spread adds richness and flavor to any ole dry piece of toast!

2 cups shredded vegan extra-sharp Cheddar cheese
8 ounces vegan cream cheese (I like Tofutti or Violife)
½ cup vegan mayonnaise (I like Best Foods or use your favorite brand)
¼ teaspoon garlic powder
¼ teaspoon cayenne pepper
¼ teaspoon onion powder
1 jalapeño pepper, seeded and minced
1 (4-ounce) jar pimiento peppers, drained and diced
1 teaspoon sea salt
½ teaspoon freshly ground black pepper

1. In a small mixing bowl, place the Cheddar, cream cheese, mayo, garlic powder, cayenne pepper, onion powder, jalapeño, pimiento peppers, salt, and black pepper. Mix all the ingredients until well combined. Store in the fridge for a few days.

Coconut Cheesecake Butter

MAKES ABOUT 2 CUPS

Yes, that's coconut *and* cheesecake *and* butter—because these things should go together and get in our bellies! Use this butter for Sunday brunch French toast or on any lowly Monday morning piece of toast with tea.

1 cup plant butter
¼ cup vegan cream cheese
½ cup powdered sugar
¼ cup coconut cream (the thick kind)
1½ teaspoons coconut extract
1 teaspoon vanilla extract

1. Using an electric mixer, whip the butter and cream cheese for 3–4 minutes until they become fluffy and light. When lots of peaks form, use a strainer to sift in the powdered sugar. Add the coconut cream, coconut extract, and vanilla extract and mix until combined. It will be a little soft and will keep in the fridge for about as long as butter will.

Sweet Skillet Southern Fried Apples

MAKES ABOUT 2 CUPS

These apples are one of my mom's favorite sweet things to have as a side, and I always really liked them too. I put my own little spin on her recipe and have added caramel for just a tad more decadence. While my mom used to make these for breakfast all the time, you can have these on ice cream or as a cake topper too.

¼ cup plant butter
4 Granny Smith or tart apples, cored and sliced ¼ inch thick
⅓ teaspoon or more cinnamon
½ cup caramel sauce (I like Mr. Dewie's or Hey Boo)

1. Heat a large skillet on medium-high heat and melt the butter. Add the apples and sauté until caramelized, for 5–7 minutes, or until just tender. Season with cinnamon and add caramel sauce. Cook for another minute or so until the apples are tender but not mushy. Remove from the heat and serve warm.

Plain Chia Pudding

MAKES 2 CUPS

These tiny mighty seeds provide so many benefits. They are loaded with omega-3 fatty acids, antioxidants, and fiber. When consumed regularly, their powerful antioxidants may help prevent heart disease. Chia seeds are also exceptionally rich in fiber, and increased fiber intake can help lower blood pressure and cholesterol levels. In addition, the essential fats help with brain development, eyesight, and concentration and boost the immune system. I can't say enough good things about this superfood. The seeds are excellent for children as well. Other recipes in this book use Plain Chia Pudding as an ingredient. You can also add berries, nut butter, chopped nuts, or whatever you want for a great breakfast or anytime pudding.

2 tablespoons chia seeds
1½ cups water or plant milk

1. Place the chia seeds and water in a bowl and stir to mix well. Or put the ingredients in an airtight container and shake until well incorporated. Let the mixture set for a couple of hours or overnight (recommended) until you get a thick chia pudding. The thickened chia seeds will grow eight times in size, and you will have 2 full cups.

Garlic Bread

MAKES ABOUT 1½ CUPS BUTTER

Who does not like garlic bread?! With this simple tasty butter, homemade garlic bread will be your new favorite thing to make. The butter will keep in the fridge for a week or so, but it won't last that long: you will find yourself spreading it on toast for a yummy snack.

1 cup plant butter, room temperature
1 tablespoon minced fresh garlic
¼ cup grated vegan Parmesan cheese
1 tablespoon garlic salt
1 teaspoon Italian seasoning
½ teaspoon freshly ground black pepper
¼ teaspoon paprika
1 large artisan bread loaf or a couple of demi baguettes, sliced

1. In an electric mixer, place the butter and whip until it is light and fluffy. Then, fold in the garlic, Parmesan, garlic salt, Italian seasoning, black pepper, and paprika. Spread the butter on fresh bread, and toast the slices under a broiler for 2–3 minutes. Serve warm and enjoy.

Everyday Italian Salad

MAKES 2 SERVINGS

I really like the simplicity of this clean, bright salad. I always have these ingredients on hand, so it's super easy to throw this salad together. Feel free to use large tomatoes or yellow onion, or whatever you have in your fridge.

5–6 ounces salad greens (your favorite kind of lettuce)
¼ small red onion, thinly sliced
1 cup cherry tomatoes
½ cup grated vegan Parmesan cheese (more if you like it extra cheesy!)
¼ cup sliced pepperoncini peppers (more if you like peppers!)
1 cup Parmesan Herb Croutons (page 29)

FOR THE QUICK DRESSING

½ cup olive oil
2 tablespoons white wine vinegar
½ teaspoon chopped fresh garlic
½ teaspoon chopped fresh parsley
½ teaspoon sea salt
Generous pinch of freshly ground black pepper
1 tablespoon grated vegan Parmesan cheese (optional—add if you're feeling extra decadent!)

1. Mix all the salad ingredients in a large bowl. For the dressing, place all the ingredients in a jar and shake vigorously. Dress the salad and top with a generous amount of Parmesan, if using. The dressing will keep for a few days in the fridge.

Tostones

MAKES 12–16 TOSTONES

Tostones are twice-fried plantain slices. As a starchy side, they're a notch up from french fries, and I love to eat them with my Blackened Tofu Grinders (page 90). No sammie? No problem. These are great as a snack with a side of Papa's Sammie Sauce (page 13).

- 2 green plantains
- 1 cup vegetable or canola oil, or as needed
- 2 teaspoons kosher or larger flake salt (optional)

1. Line a plate with paper towels and set aside.

2. Trim and discard the ends of the plantains. Use a knife to cut a slit along the length of each plantain to easily remove the peels. Slice each plantain crosswise into 6–8 pieces. In a large skillet, place about ½ inch of oil and fry the plantains until golden-brown on the bottom, for 2–3 minutes. Flip and repeat on the other side.

3. Once the plantain slices are golden but still firm, transfer them to a cutting board and smash each slice with the bottom of a jar or the flat side of a sturdy spatula. Don't smash too hard or the slices will break. Return each mashed slice to the hot oil and fry until slightly crisp.

4. Transfer to the paper towel–lined plate to drain a bit. Season with salt, if desired, and serve.

Tangy Skillet BBQ Beans

MAKES 4 SERVINGS

These beans have a lovely sweet tangy flavor with a subtle smokiness. A chef I met on the road in Arkansas at this amazing hotel introduced me to this BBQ bean recipe. The hotel had an entire department of chefs who created special meals to serve on the hotel's own in-house aircraft, and this was one of them. And when I tell you these guys could cook—man, oh man! These simple and delicious beans go great with sandwiches and burgers.

- 3 tablespoons avocado oil
- ½ cup minced Baba's Mesquite Smoked Tofu or tempeh bacon
- 1 cup diced bell or mini sweet peppers
- ¾ cup diced yellow onion
- 1½ teaspoons chopped fresh garlic
- ½ cup white wine
- ½ cup BBQ sauce (I like Stubbs Original or use your favorite BBQ sauce)
- 6 tablespoons agave
- 2 tablespoons cider vinegar
- ½ tablespoon liquid mesquite smoke (I like Stubbs)
- 2 (15-ounce) cans cannellini beans or white beans, rinsed and drained
- 1 teaspoon sea salt
- Generous pinch of freshly ground black pepper
- 2–3 tablespoons plant butter (I like Country Crock)

1. Heat a medium saucepan on medium high with avocado oil. Add the tofu, peppers, onion, and garlic; they should sizzle when they hit the pan. Cook on high for 3–5 minutes until everything is very fragrant and turning dark golden-brown.

2. Deglaze with the wine: allow the wine to cook off for about 5 minutes. Turn the heat down to a simmer.

3. In a mixing bowl, combine the BBQ sauce, agave, vinegar, and liquid smoke. Pour this mixture into the veggie mixture in the pan. Add the beans, season with salt and pepper, and cook for about 15 minutes, or until the beans split. Finish by adding butter and giving a stir to combine. Serve with my Tofu Bacon, Lettuce, and Tomato Sammie (page 97) or your favorite sammie.

Good Morning Goodness

As I traveled the nation and the world on the *Songs in the Key of Life* tour as Stevie Wonder's personal chef, I learned how to nourish myself. I learned to become an early riser to prep my day, and as I worked in the kitchen, I always took a moment to make myself something nice to eat. I became really curious about different types of granolas, and I explored many ways of making breakfast sandwiches and warm oatmeal and grain bowls. I share here just a tad of what we ate on the road.

This section provides options for everyone, whether you are grabbing a quick bite as you dash out the door to catch a plane or rush to the office, or have time for a more leisurely meal. Maybe you're a morning juice kinda gal or guy, or maybe you like quinoa or French toast for breakfast, like I do. Either way, this section has variety. The first part provides plenty of easy recipes for quick nourishment on the weekdays, while the second part helps you create tasty, lazy weekend breakfasts for the whole family.

WEEKDAY BREAKFAST

While I am largely a savory breakfast person, I like to make sure to have both sweet and savory breakfast options when I am cooking in my restaurant or for private clients. And that goes for these recipes too. These sweet and savory breakfast items are so good, you won't want to skip the most important meal of the day. I believe that breakfast should be just as interesting as lunch and supper. No matter if you prefer fresh juices, rice and beans, or cereal, these weekday recipes will start your day with a happy belly.

The Incredible Hulk

MAKES ABOUT 2 CUPS

This glass of greens will supercharge your day, and if you drink it consistently, you will feel pretty incredible. When I drink this, I'm not hungry for hours, and I really think I can feel the nutrients and hydration; it's like having an ultrapowerful multivitamin. This drink will flush the toxins right out of your system.

1½-inch piece fresh ginger
1½-inch piece fresh turmeric
½ bunch spinach
½ bunch green kale
3 ribs celery
1 cucumber

1. Using your favorite extractor juicer, put the ginger and turmeric in first, then the spinach and kale, followed by the celery ribs, and finally the entire cucumber. Serve over ice.

Orange Sunrise

MAKES ABOUT 2 CUPS

I cannot say enough good about a glass of veggie juice. I drink this particular one when I need some good body soothing. The turmeric helps with inflammation while the ginger is loaded with antioxidants that help prevent stress and damage to your DNA. The rest of the ingredients are equally powerful. Add 2–3 cloves of garlic, known for fighting bacteria, viruses, fungi, and parasites, and they will help to knock out any cold or flu. For an even more pumped-up boost, add hot pepper.

1½-inch piece fresh turmeric
1½-inch piece fresh ginger
1 large or 2 small golden beets
1 bunch carrots (about 6)

1. Using your favorite extractor juicer, put the turmeric and ginger in first, then the golden beets. Remove the greens from the carrots and juice last. Serve over ice.

Strawberry Chia Power Smoothie

MAKES 1 LARGE GLASS OR 2 SMALL GLASSES

I really love the efficiency of drinking breakfast! You can pack so many nutrients into a glass. The base here is strawberries and bananas with a chia pudding; you'll need to make the pudding ahead of time. Chia seeds aren't just for chia pets; they contain large amounts of fiber and omega-3 fatty acids, plenty of high-quality protein, and several essential minerals and antioxidants. The other ingredients are just as healthy. The good news is that you can use whatever fruit you have on hand. I really love the sweet tanginess of this combo, but try mixing and matching your fruits however you like. Whatever you use, keep the chia, and don't worry: no one will ever know there is chia in the smoothie!

1 cup frozen strawberries
1 medium banana
½ cup Plain Chia Pudding (page 33)
½ cup orange juice
1 cup almond milk
1 tablespoon agave (optional)

1. Place all the ingredients in a blender and blend until smooth.

The Blacker the Berry . . .

MAKES 1 LARGE GLASS OR 2 SMALL GLASSES

This mixture of blackberries, pineapple, and coconut creates a unique and refreshing flavor profile that is both sweet and tangy, with a tropical twist. If you ask me, pineapple is like the secret weapon of smoothies; its undercover citrus notes excite anything you add it to. It's also not too shabby in the nutrient department, with a high vitamin and mineral content that promotes tissue healing, fights inflammation, aids digestion, and helps with arthritis pain relief. But the real star here is the mighty blackberry: packed with vitamin C and fiber, blackberries help keep your brain healthy. Make sure to get the thick coconut cream for this smoothie; it adds a smooth yumminess.

1 cup frozen pineapple
1 cup frozen blackberries
½ cup thick coconut cream (the canned milk kind)
1 cup orange juice
¼ cup or more Plain Chia Pudding (page 33)
1 tablespoon agave (optional)

1. In a bullet or blender, place the pineapple, blackberries, coconut cream, orange juice, chia pudding, and agave, if using. Blend all the ingredients until very smooth.

Costa Rican Rice and Bean Bowl

MAKES 4 SERVINGS

If you like a sweet breakfast and are skeptical about a savory one, this bowl is the best of both worlds: the beans and rice are a hearty foundation, and the plantains add a sweet note. When picking plantains, I like them to be right at the edge of ripeness, slightly soft with a rich golden-yellow color. If you like them supersweet, you can go as far as the black ones.

FOR THE BOWL BASE

Avocado oil for cooking
1 green bell pepper or 4 multicolored sweet mini peppers, diced
½ cup diced yellow onion
1 teaspoon chopped fresh garlic
2 cups cooked white rice
1 (15-ounce) can black beans, rinsed and drained
½ teaspoon cumin
½ teaspoon sea salt
½ teaspoon freshly ground black pepper
½ cup chopped fresh cilantro

FOR THE TOPPINGS

3 tablespoons avocado oil, divided
1 cup JUST Egg
2 ripe plantains
2 ripe avocados, sliced or diced
3 limes, cut into wedges
3 tablespoons chopped fresh cilantro leaves
3 Roma tomatoes, diced
Hot sauce (your favorite smoky sauce, optional but recommended)

1. To make the rice and beans, heat the oil over high heat in a large nonstick skillet and add the peppers, onion, and garlic. Sauté until soft, for about 3 minutes (you still want the veggies bright). Reduce the heat to medium. Add the rice and black beans and cook, stirring occasionally, until everything is heated through, for 2–3 more minutes. Season with cumin, salt, and pepper, and stir until fragrant. Turn off the heat and mix in the chopped cilantro. Remove the mixture from the pan and keep it warm.

2. To make the egg and plantains, use the same pan coated with a bit of oil. Cook the JUST Egg according to the package directions (see Pan-Fried Eggs on page 63). Slice the ripe plantains diagonally, ½–¾ inch thick. In the same skillet, heat more avocado oil. When the oil is hot, place the plantain slices in a single layer and cook until they start to brown and become caramelized and soft, for 2–3 minutes. Flip and cook for an additional 2–3 minutes on the other side. Remove and place on a plate (no paper towel!).

3. To assemble, put a generous amount of bean and rice mixture into each bowl. Top with egg, plantains, avocado slices, lime wedges, cilantro, Roma tomatoes, and hot sauce.

Baba's Morning Quinoa

MAKES 4 SERVINGS

I am trying out new recipes all the time. This is definitely one I would have tried out on my dad. He loved my creative cooking, and I'm pretty confident he would have loved this dish. I can say, hands down, this is one of my more creative breakfast ideas: it mixes a lot of textures, some maybe not as familiar as others. The most exciting thing about this bowl is the mixture of the yogurt sauce, pesto, and egg. The flavors and textures add up to a complex, yummy combination that is a pleasant surprise.

1 cup plain, unsweetened cashew yogurt (I like Forager)
1 tablespoon chopped fresh cilantro
1 tablespoon chopped fresh mint or parsley leaves
Salt and pepper
1 teaspoon flaky regular salt and pinch of curry (optional)
1 cup JUST Egg
Generous pinch or more of curry powder (optional)
Avocado oil for cooking
½ pound tofu, cut into ½-inch cubes (I like Baba's Tofustrami or use your favorite savory tofu)
2 cups cooked, multicolored quinoa
¼ cup Fresh Cilantro Pesto (page 15)
1 cup shredded fresh baby spinach
1 avocado, sliced
4 lemon wedges

1. In a medium bowl, mix the cashew yogurt, cilantro, mint, and a pinch each of salt and pepper. Stir until combined. Set aside in the fridge.
2. To make the curry salt, add a generous pinch of curry to 1 teaspoon of flaky salt.
3. In a small mixing bowl, add the JUST Egg, a generous pinch of salt, a pinch of black pepper, and curry powder, if using.
4. Heat a nonstick pan to medium heat and put in a tablespoon or more of avocado oil.
5. Add the cubes of tofu and cook until the tofu crispens up, stirring to ensure it browns on all sides, for 3–4 minutes. Remove from the pan with a slotted spoon. Add the egg to the pan and cook for 1–2 minutes until it starts to bubble in the center and brown on the bottom. Flip and allow to cook to a firmness you like (I like to have the egg in larger pieces).
6. Split the quinoa among four bowls and add a large spoonful of yogurt sauce to each bowl. Swirl a spoonful of pesto into the yogurt sauce, and add the tofu, egg, spinach, and avocado. Serve with a wedge of lemon, and season with curry salt, if you like.

Fruity Chia Yogurt Bowls with Toasted Granola

MAKES 2–3 SERVINGS

A good morning starts with a happy belly. Yogurt and chia make a powerful combination loaded with minerals, nutrients, fiber, and protein, not to mention belly-calming probiotics. I add mango, kiwi, and blueberry, but you can mix and match your fruits however you like. Top with a yummy granola, and you've got a nutritious, delicious good morning hug for your belly!

2 cups or more plain, unsweetened nondairy yogurt, divided (I like Forager)
½ cup Plain Chia Pudding (page 33)
2 tablespoons or more agave
½ mango, peeled and diced
½ cup blueberries
1 kiwi, peeled and sliced
1 cup toasted granola (your favorite store-bought brand)

1. Split the yogurt between two bowls. Add ¼ cup of chia pudding to each bowl and mix well to combine. Drizzle agave on top. Create a pretty arrangement for your bowls by topping each with half the mango, blueberries, kiwi, and granola.

WEEKEND BREAKFAST

I shied away from calling this section "brunch" because brunch often feels like more of an event than we may be up for. Now, you can make these things for a holiday or special event brunch, but they are also perfect for any ole weekend you feel like treating yourself and the ones you love.

Good Morning Breakfast Tacos

You will be in a taco coma after you eat these, I promise. Each one is a different level of taco yumminess packed with a variety of plant meats and cheeses. Try the trio or try three of one—you can't go wrong.

Bacon and Scrambled Egg Tacos

MAKES 4 TACOS

Tofu is one of the most adaptable, clean, and unprocessed plant proteins I have worked with. While it is pretty much the original "plant meat" (it dates back two thousand years!), some folks still think tofu is weird. I love to create dishes that make eating tofu easy and everyday. This is just one of them.

2 tablespoons or more avocado oil
¼ pound or more Baba's Mesquite Smoked Tofu or LightLife Tempeh Smoky Bacon
1 cup or more JUST Egg
4 (6-inch) corn tortillas
1 avocado, sliced
¼ cup pico de gallo (page 25)
Vegan Parmesan cheese, grated, for garnish
Fresh cilantro, chopped, for garnish
Lime slices, for garnish

1. If using Baba's Mesquite Smoked Tofu, slice it thin, like bacon, into 8–10 strips. Heat a pan and place a bit of oil in the bottom. Add the tofu to the pan and fry until crispy, for 2–3 minutes, depending on how hot the pan is.

2. Remove from the heat and set aside. Wipe the pan and put in a little more avocado oil. Add JUST Egg and cook according to the package directions or scramble as you would a traditional egg, stirring occasionally (see Pan-Fried Eggs on page 63). Wait until the egg begins to set. I like this mixture to be a tad drier than a traditional egg.

3. Heat a nonstick pan over medium heat. Put in the tortillas and warm them, for a minute or less on each side. Remove the tortillas from the pan and transfer them to a clean plate; cover to keep warm.

4. To build tacos: divide the egg mixture into four servings, putting about ¼ cup on each tortilla, and then add the crumbled tofu, avocado slices, and pico de gallo. Garnish with Parmesan and cilantro. Serve with lime slices for an extra kick.

Spicy Sausage and Hash Browns Tacos

MAKES 6–8 TACOS

This taco is satisfying; it's meaty and robust. I'm a two-taco kinda gal, but you do you.

1 pound bag store-bought country-style shredded potatoes (I like Kroger)
1 (14-ounce) package Impossible Sausage (you can use the savory, but I like the spicy)
6–8 (6-inch) tortillas
2 avocados, sliced vertically, 3–4 slices per quarter
4 cups pico de gallo (page 25)
1 serving Pepper Pot Pickled Onions (page 25)
Fresh cilantro, chopped, for garnish
Lime wedges, for garnish

1. Cook the hash brown potatoes according to the package directions, making sure to get them crispy. Set aside, covered to keep warm.

2. Heat a medium skillet or pan to medium heat and put in the Impossible Sausage. Cook until it browns and firms up, for 2–3 minutes per side. Remove from the pan and keep warm.

3. Warm the tortillas in batches, placing 1–2 tortillas in the pan and warming them about a minute on each side. Transfer to a plate, keeping them under a towel or another plate to keep warm as you work.

4. Assemble the tacos: lay the tortillas out and divide the hash browns among them. Spoon about 3 tablespoons or as much sausage as you like on each tortilla. Top with 3 slices of avocado, then about 2 tablespoons or more of pico de gallo and a few pepper pot onions. Garnish with cilantro and serve with lime for a little extra zest.

Plant Beef and Cheese Taquitos with Queso Sauce

MAKES 8 TAQUITOS

Crunchy, cheesy, meaty: three words that mean "hearty, yummy, satisfying" or "perfect cure for a hangover"!

8 (6-inch) corn tortillas
1 (14-ounce) package plant sausage (Impossible Sausage, spicy)
Cooking oil for frying
1 serving Pimiento Cheese (page 31)
4 cups pico de gallo (page 25)
1 avocado, sliced

1. Line a half-size baking sheet or large plate with paper towels and set aside.
2. Heat a medium pan to medium-high heat; put in as many tortillas as will fit and cook for 2–3 minutes on each side until warm. Place them on a plate and cover to keep warm.
3. Place Impossible Sausage in the pan and cook until it browns, for 2–3 minutes. Remove from the pan and set aside.
4. Wipe the pan clean, fill with cooking oil about two-thirds full, and heat the oil over medium high. Working in batches, take one tortilla and fill it with as much sausage as will fit, about 3 tablespoons, and roll tightly; pin with a toothpick. Repeat with all the tortillas.
5. When ready to cook, place the stuffed tortillas in the pan seam side down; they should sizzle as they hit the pan. Cook until golden-brown, for 2–3 minutes, and then rotate to cook on all sides until golden-brown. Remove from the pan and transfer to the paper towel–lined tray to drain. If a pan of hot boiling oil makes you nervous, you can try these in the air fryer. (I have not tried an air fryer because I like to live on the edge!)
6. Drizzle the cheese sauce over each taquito, and top with pico de gallo and a side of avocado.

Summerland
Sweets
Strawberry Syrup

Sunday Morning Celebration

Stevie *loved* brunch any day of the week. When we were out on the road, this breakfast of French toast, tofu scramble, skillet potatoes, and sausage was a morning celebration whenever we had downtime. I would make this spread for Stevie when we had a few days in a city, or when he would invite his friends over and the next day wasn't a travel day. It does not have to be on a Sunday, but if you have the time on a Sunday, put on a pot of coffee and roll up your sleeves: this brunch has a lot of moving parts, but it's so worth it.

Salted Caramel French Toast with Skillet Spiced Apples

MAKES 3–4 SERVINGS

This is next-level French toast. I like JUST Egg here: it gives you that nice eggy batter to coat the bread nicely. Add extra-creamy oat milk for extra richness. You are going to be so proud of yourself when you make this: the flavors are so smooth together!

FOR THE SKILLET SPICED APPLES

2 large Granny Smith or other tart apples
3–4 tablespoons cooking oil (avocado, safflower, or canola)
2–3 slices tofu (I like Baba's Mesquite Smoked Tofu or LightLife Tempeh Smoky Bacon)
½ cup natural cane sugar
½ teaspoon cinnamon
½ teaspoon nutmeg
1 teaspoon vanilla extract
Pinch of sea salt

FOR THE FRENCH TOAST

1 cup oat milk (I like Chobani Extra Creamy)
1 cup JUST Egg
1 teaspoon vanilla extract
6–8 slices of bread or more
¼ cup or more cooking oil (avocado, safflower, or canola)

1. Cut the apples in quarters and core the seeds. Cut each quarter vertically into slices, about ¼ inch thick. Line a plate with paper towels and set aside.
2. Heat a skillet over medium-high heat with cooking oil; once hot, add the tofu bacon and fry until crispy, about 2 minutes. Remove from the oil and set aside on the paper towel–lined plate.
3. Add the apples to the hot oil; they should sizzle as they hit the hot oil. Season with sugar, cinnamon, nutmeg, vanilla extract, and salt. Cover with a lid and reduce the heat a bit. Cook until the apples start to soften, caramelize, and create their own syrup, for 2–3 minutes. Lower heat and cook for another 6–8 minutes until the apples start to reduce in size.
4. Add the tofu bacon back in. The apples will be slightly soft but still have their shape.
5. While the apples are cooking, prep the French toast. In a medium bowl, combine the milk, egg, and vanilla extract, and mix. Lay each slice of bread in the egg mixture and flip to coat both sides; remove and set aside.
6. Heat a nonstick pan with cooking oil. Working in batches, pan-fry the slices on each side until golden-brown and slightly crispy on the edges. Keep them warm in the oven.

Tofu Egg Scramble

MAKES 4 SERVINGS

This was one of Stevie's favorite things for breakfast on the road; he called it "tofu egg." With a ton of veggies and tofu, this is your classic scramble. The key here is the type of tofu you use; my go-to is Trader Joe's. If it's available, I use the basic tofu with the hot-pink label. If you can't find that, use any regular (not soft) tofu.

¼ cup avocado oil
1 cup chopped oyster mushrooms
¼ cup diced yellow onion
¼ cup diced red or any color bell pepper
1 teaspoon chopped fresh garlic
1 (14-ounce) package tofu (I like Trader Joe's)
3–4 tablespoons tamari
Generous pinch of freshly ground black pepper
¼ teaspoon chili flakes
2 generous tablespoons fresh herbs (I like parsley, but you can use dill, rosemary, thyme—whatever you like.)

1. Heat a skillet or pan with the avocado oil to medium high. Add the mushrooms, onion, peppers, and garlic and sauté for 2 minutes, or until the vegetables start to soften and brown.
2. While the veggies are cooking, drain the water from the tofu. Once the veggies start to become fragrant, in about 2 minutes, use your hands to crumble the tofu into the pan in random large pieces. Using a soft spatula, gently fold the tofu in with the veggies, making sure not to break the tofu up too much.
3. Allow to cook for another 2–3 minutes, to cook some of the water off, then add the tamari and season with black pepper and chili flakes. Cook for another couple of minutes or so (I like my tofu a little bit drier), allowing the tamari to brown and stick to the pan and the tofu.
4. Add the herbs and remove from heat. Serve immediately.

Skillet Breakfast Potatoes

MAKES 4 SERVINGS

My mom says you can't have breakfast without a good potato, and I agree! We made skillet potatoes all the time when I was a kid. Here's my grown-up version, which has a little heat from the Cajun seasoning. Serve this with any sweet or savory breakfast.

3 tablespoons avocado oil or more if you like
4 cups diced potatoes with skin on (2–3, depending on size)
1 teaspoon chopped fresh garlic
½ cup or more coarsely diced yellow onion
2 teaspoons fresh thyme
½ teaspoon sea salt
¼ teaspoon freshly ground black pepper
¼ teaspoon onion powder
3½ teaspoons Cajun seasoning
Pinch of chili flakes
1 tablespoon chopped fresh parsley

1. Heat a skillet on medium high with the avocado oil. Add the potatoes and spread across the bottom of the pan. Put the garlic and onions on top; cover and cook for about 5 minutes, giving a stir once or twice. When the potatoes start to brown but are still very firm, season with thyme, salt, pepper, onion powder, Cajun seasoning, and chili flakes.

2. Cover again and allow to cook at medium heat; the potatoes will turn golden-brown and stick to the bottom of the pan. Using a flat flapjack flipper or spatula, lift the cover and flip the potatoes occasionally as they cook. Cook for about 20 minutes, until they have softened and have a nice crispy crust. Garnish with fresh parsley.

COOK'S NOTE: You'll want to use a flat flapjack flipper because the potatoes will stick, and this thin spatula will help you get them off the pan.

Breakfast Sausage

MAKES 4–6 PATTIES

There are lots of store-bought, premade, plant-based breakfast sausages these days, and if you have some in your freezer, go ahead and use them. But if you want some extra flavor, try this recipe: it is super quick, and you can make it ahead and keep it in the freezer.

1 pound ground plant beef (I like Before the Butcher Uncut Burger or Beyond Burger)
¼ cup chopped onion
2 tablespoons maple syrup
½ tablespoon chopped fresh garlic
1½ tablespoons chopped fresh sage
½ tablespoon chopped fresh thyme leaves
1 teaspoon chopped fresh parsley
1 teaspoon sea salt
1 teaspoon freshly ground black pepper
¼ teaspoon paprika
Pinch of cayenne pepper

1. In a mixing bowl, place the plant meat, onion, maple syrup, garlic, sage, thyme, parsley, salt and pepper, paprika, and cayenne. Mix until well combined and then shape into patties 1½–2 inches around. (At this point, you can freeze them to cook later; they will keep a good two weeks.) When ready to use, heat a pan to medium heat and cook the patties for 2–3 minutes on each side, or until the meat firms up. Serve with your favorite breakfast, make into a sammie, or eat as a snack! If you don't have time for this entire recipe, I also like MorningStar Farms Sausage Patties.

Southern Saturday Morning

I still remember those lazy weekends when we lived in Alabama and the weather had gotten just a little chilly so we couldn't drive to Pensacola to the beach. My parents would be in the kitchen cooking up a storm, my mom with her breakfast potatoes and crunchy pan-fried tofu bacon and my dad with his grits and grease. My dad, whom we called Baba, would always make some biscuits, not measuring a thing, and they would always turn out perfect. My parents always had something sweet too, like pan-fried apples. I hope this makes your weekends just as sweet and lazy as ours were.

Along with the recipes below, make a batch of Warm Butter Biscuits (page 116), Sweet Skillet Southern Fried Apples (page 32), and Skillet Breakfast Potatoes (page 59) to complete your southern Saturday morning.

Pan-Fried Eggs

MAKES 4 SERVINGS

The new egg analogues are game changers. I use JUST Egg to mix things up a bit. The following recipe is one way I cook eggs. Make sure to grab a little black Himalayan salt, also called sulfur salt, and season to your taste; it will add an eggy flavor.

Avocado oil for cooking
1 cup JUST Egg
Sulfur salt (optional)
Black pepper, freshly ground

1. I like to scramble my JUST Egg according to the package directions. Preheat a small nonstick skillet over medium to medium-high heat and coat evenly with a bit of oil.
2. Shake the bottle of JUST Egg well. Pour the desired amount into the skillet. Shimmy the skillet to distribute the liquid evenly, and let it sit for a moment before stirring.
3. Scramble like an egg: use a spatula to occasionally scrape and pull the mixture across the pan while still letting the JUST Egg heat evenly and set. Steadily push the cooked sections out from the center and edges and redistribute the remaining liquid across the pan. When the liquid is about halfway cooked through, add any vegetables or desired additions. Scramble until all the liquid is just cooked through. Use the spatula to break the scramble up into fluffy, bite-size pieces. Remove from the heat.
4. Sprinkle the cooked scramble with sulfur salt, if desired, and black pepper to taste.

Tofu Bacon or Tempeh Bacon

MAKES 4 SERVINGS

1 package Baba's Mesquite Smoked Tofu or LightLife Tempeh Smoky Bacon
2 tablespoons cooking oil (avocado, safflower, or canola)

1. If you are using Baba's Mesquite Smoked Tofu, slice it thin like bacon and pan-fry on medium-high heat with a little cooking oil for 1–2 per side. If you are using LightLife tempeh, pan-fry with oil for about 2 minutes per side. LightLife won't crisp the same way as Baba's, but it will turn golden and very fragrant.

Grits and Grease

MAKES 4 SERVINGS

My father grew up in the stunning countryside of Alabama, and one of his favorite foods was grits. My dad would always tell us stories about Aunt TT or Paw Paw or Sambo or some other larger-than-life character. Those stories always had a food element to them, whether it was the kids becoming excited about getting their grandparents' watermelon rinds or Aunt TT's cooking, and grits and grease were front and center. Many of us know what grits are and have our own opinions of yellow or white (I am team white), but adding flavored drippings from the pan is what really makes them taste great. This recipe uses tofu bacon drippings to flavor the grits, for a plant twist on a good ole southern fave.

2 cups water
½ teaspoon kosher salt
½ cup quick grits (not instant)
½ cup shredded vegan sharp Cheddar cheese or whatever cheese you like
1 tablespoon or more bacon bits and bacon oil (page 21), per serving

1. Bring the water to a boil in a small saucepan. Then add the salt and quick grits. Stir or whisk to combine. Allow to return to a boil and then reduce the heat to medium low and cook for 8–10 minutes.
2. Make sure to stir the grits often while cooking them. When the grits are done, add the cheese and mix until it is melted.
3. Remove the pan from the heat and serve immediately with crumbled tofu bacon and bacon oil.

Simple Lunches and Anytime Meals

I love a tasty side dish and so does Stevie. He is a man who enjoys a light lunch or a good snack for those in-between times, and if you do too, what better way to enjoy a tasty little something than to make it light and bright or fresh and crunchy. These lovely treats of meals will satisfy you, whether or not you are vegan.

Plum Bistro is my part of our family business, a business we have had in our family for more than fifty years. My mother—a super badass lady—launched the food portion of our business with a sandwich company. Her bright ideas and innovation met an untapped, hungry market: she hit the local scene with a splash. It was the first tofu sandwich company in the region, maybe even in the nation, and she started it while homeschooling us. After she and my dad made the commitment to veganism, her number one priority was having something good to eat. So they set about creating a new taste, largely with tofu, tempeh, seitan, and even quinoa, before quinoa was the huge craze it is now.

So I'm just going to say it: I am really good at soups and sandwiches. I love this simply good section of the food universe. You can make so many things yummier by putting them between two slices of bread—and then add a steaming hot bowl of goodness to eat with them. Heaven.

Citrus Black-Eyed Pea Salad with Sweet Cornbread

MAKES 4 SERVINGS

When I was on the road with Stevie, I started to look for new ways of cooking. We had to move so quickly from city to city, cooking what was available really became a thing. I think I really started to fall in love with food while I was on the road. There were times we would land in the middle of the night, and I had to use whatever was available in the hotel kitchen—in the night cook's pantry and the walk-in refrigerator. I like this salad because it is a light riff on a southern legume staple and easy on the body to eat anytime. It's bright, citrusy, and full of fiber, and the cornbread adds a sweet comforting note to round this salad out as a tasty small meal.

Box Cornbread/Muffins (page 30)
2 (15-ounce) cans black-eyed peas, rinsed and drained
1 cup diced sweet peppers, cut into ¼-inch pieces
1 cup cherry tomatoes, quartered
1 cup or more Fresh Herb Oil (page 20)
¼ cup diced red onion
½ cup minced cilantro
3 tablespoons freshly squeezed lemon juice
1 tablespoon cider vinegar
1 tablespoon diced jalapeño pepper (optional)
½ teaspoon lemon zest
1½ teaspoons sea salt
½ teaspoon freshly ground black pepper

1. Make the cornbread according to the instructions on page 30. While it is baking, prepare the salad. In a salad bowl, place the black-eyed peas, sweet peppers, tomatoes, herb oil, and onion. Season with cilantro, lemon juice, cider vinegar, jalapeño (if desired), lemon zest, salt, and black pepper. Mix all the ingredients until well combined. Serve with the warm cornbread.

Middle Eastern–Inspired Chickpea Salad with Grilled Pita

MAKES 2 SERVINGS

A few years ago I was a plant-based food consultant for the Google campuses in Seattle, and I got to make really tasty, plant-based meals to integrate into Google's food system. This is one of the salads that I made: the chickpeas, cucumber, and tomatoes combined with fresh herbs make a meal all by themselves. If you want more protein, serve this, as I did at Google, with the Portobello Gyros (page 95).

FOR THE SALAD

1 (32-ounce) can chickpeas
2 cups diced Roma tomatoes, cut into ½-inch cubes
2 cups diced English cucumber, cut into ½-inch cubes, or about 1 large cucumber
¾ cup very thinly sliced purple onion
½ cup chopped fresh parsley
1 teaspoon chopped fresh dill

FOR THE DRESSING

1 tablespoon chopped fresh garlic
⅓ cup freshly squeezed lime juice, or juice of about 3 limes
½ cup olive oil
2 teaspoons sea salt
½ teaspoon freshly ground black pepper

FOR THE PITA

2 store-bought pita breads
1 tablespoon Fresh Herb Oil (page 20)
Flaky salt and pepper
Fresh herbs, such as parsley or dill (optional)

1. Drain the chickpeas and save the liquid (called aquafaba) for later use. Place the chickpeas in a salad bowl along with the tomatoes, cucumber, onion, parsley, and dill. Add the garlic, lime juice, olive oil, salt, and pepper to the salad bowl and mix well. Set aside and let marinate while you prepare the pita.
2. Heat a pan over medium heat. Brush the pitas with herb oil and place them in the pan. Grill on each side until they are brown and toasty, for a minute or so. Remove them from the pan and brush with more herb oil, if you like, then season with flaky salt and pepper plus any herbs, if using. Serve the salad with the warm pita bread.

Calamari Lettuce Wraps

MAKES 2–3 SERVINGS

This is one of the most popular dishes at Plum Bistro. We often have half a ticket rail with just calamari orders. We serve it on a sheet tray with a pile of crispy, crunchy, slightly salty, and peppery plant calamari. The secret ingredient here is oyster mushrooms. The calamari are light and crisp but at the same time rich and dense in the right places, with just the right amount of sweet heat from the sweet chili sauce.

COOK'S NOTE: You'll need a thermometer to check the temperature of the oil.

1 cup plain, unsweetened plant milk (I like soy)
½ teaspoon cider vinegar
8 ounces oyster mushrooms
Oil for frying
2 cups Black Pepper Breading (page 16)
2–3 tablespoons Sweet Chili Sauce (page 19)
Iceberg lettuce
Cilantro, chopped
Green onion, chopped
Jalapeño pepper, chopped (optional)

1. In a small bowl, mix the milk and vinegar and let the mixture set until it thickens, for 1–2 minutes.
2. Pull the mushrooms apart until you have something resembling thick pieces of pulled pork. Layer paper towels on a plate and set aside.
3. Place the frying oil in a deep skillet until it is about ¾ inch deep. Heat until it registers 350°F on a candy thermometer. (If you don't have a thermometer, the oil will shimmer and appear much thinner when it's hot enough.)
4. While the oil is heating, prepare the Black Pepper Breading in a shallow dish. Mix it thoroughly.
5. Working in small batches at a time, dredge your mushrooms in the milk and then in the Black Pepper Breading. Once coated with breading, drop the mushrooms into the hot oil and cook until the pieces start to float and turn a rich golden-brown, for about 2 minutes. Remove from the oil and place on the paper towels.
6. I like to serve the fried mushrooms topped with a generous amount of Sweet Chili Sauce and a pile of iceberg lettuce; this crisp lettuce complements the crispy dense bites of mushroom. Garnish with cilantro, green onion, and jalapeño, if using.

General Tso Cauliflower

MAKES 3 SERVINGS

Stevie really enjoys Chinese food. He asked me to make him something good one day, and this is what I came up with. The crispy dense cauliflower stands in well for an animal protein, and the sauce is just the right amount of sweet and salty; together they are a nostalgic taste combo. I gave the dish a modern earthy twist with forbidden black rice.

FOR THE GENERAL TSO SAUCE

2½ cups water
⅓ cup soy sauce
⅔ cup rice wine vinegar
1¼ cups hoisin sauce
¼ cup Gochujang Fermented Hot Chile Paste
⅓ cup sesame oil
¼ cup cornstarch

FOR THE PANKO CAULIFLOWER

1 head cauliflower
4 cups panko breadcrumbs
2 teaspoons sea salt
2 cups soy milk
1 tablespoon vinegar
6 cups water
½ head broccoli, for garnish
4 cups frying oil
Pinch of salt

FOR THE FORBIDDEN RICE

1 cup black rice
½ teaspoon sea salt
2 cups water

1. Combine all the sauce ingredients in a blender and blend until smooth. Set aside.
2. Wash the cauliflower and pat dry. Cut into pieces. Place the panko and salt in a bowl. Whisk the soy milk and vinegar together until the mixture thickens to the texture of buttermilk. Toss the cauliflower pieces in the milk and then in the panko until coated. Place the pieces on a sheet tray so they're not touching.
3. Cook the black rice with salted water in a rice cooker.
4. Prepare the broccoli: In a pot, boil the 6 cups of water and blanch the broccoli for 30 seconds to 1 minute, depending on whether you like your broccoli crunchy or soft. I'm a crunchy gal. Once your broccoli is cooked, drain and cut it into florets, then toss with a pinch of salt.
5. Fry the cauliflower: You can air-fry or heat the frying oil in a small but deep pot to 335°F (170°C). Carefully drop the cauliflower pieces into the oil in small batches. The cauliflower should float at the top of the oil. Fry until light golden-brown, for about 5 minutes, then transfer to a cooling rack or a plate lined with paper towels to drain. Continue frying in batches.
6. Once all the cauliflower has been fried, heat the General Tso sauce in a small saucepot over medium heat until it starts to thicken. Divide the black rice into three bowls, top with the fried cauliflower, and pour the sauce over it, as much as you like. Garnish with broccoli florets.

SABRE

Savory Egg Pancake with Napa Cabbage Slaw and Steamed Rice

MAKES 4 LARGE PANCAKES

I became very curious about pickles and salts when we traveled back and forth to New York while on the *Songs in the Key of Life* tour or when Stevie had an event. We always stayed at the same hotel, and the chefs in that kitchen knew me well. Every time I would come back, they would say, "Hey, Chef, you know where everything is," along with a loud "Welcome back!"—delivered in their robust, heavy New York accent. They were experienced older cooks who really understood food. They would teach me how to use salts and pickles or aromatic spices and marinades. This is a yummy surprise of a light lunch; it was perfect for when we would land midday, just before heading to a show.

FOR THE PANCAKE

1 cup JUST Egg
¼ cup shredded carrot
1 cup shredded zucchini
¼ cup sliced green onions
¼ teaspoon sea salt
½ teaspoon freshly ground black pepper
½ teaspoon toasted sesame seeds (optional)
Cooking oil (avocado, safflower, or canola)

FOR THE PANCAKE DIPPING SAUCE

1 tablespoon sriracha
2 tablespoons soy sauce or tamari
1 tablespoon water
¼ teaspoon toasted sesame seeds
1 tablespoon sesame oil
2 teaspoons rice vinegar
½ teaspoon light-brown sugar
1 tablespoon sliced green onion, plus more for garnish

1. In a mixing bowl, combine the egg, carrot, zucchini, and green onion and season with salt, pepper, and sesame seeds, if using.
2. In a small bowl, mix the sriracha, soy sauce, water, sesame seeds, sesame oil, rice vinegar, brown sugar, and green onion.
3. Coat a nonstick pan with a thin layer of cooking oil and heat on medium-high heat. Drop in the pancake mixture. You can make one large Asian-style savory pancake or several small ones. Cook on each side until golden-brown, for 2–3 minutes per side. Serve with the dipping sauce and green onions.

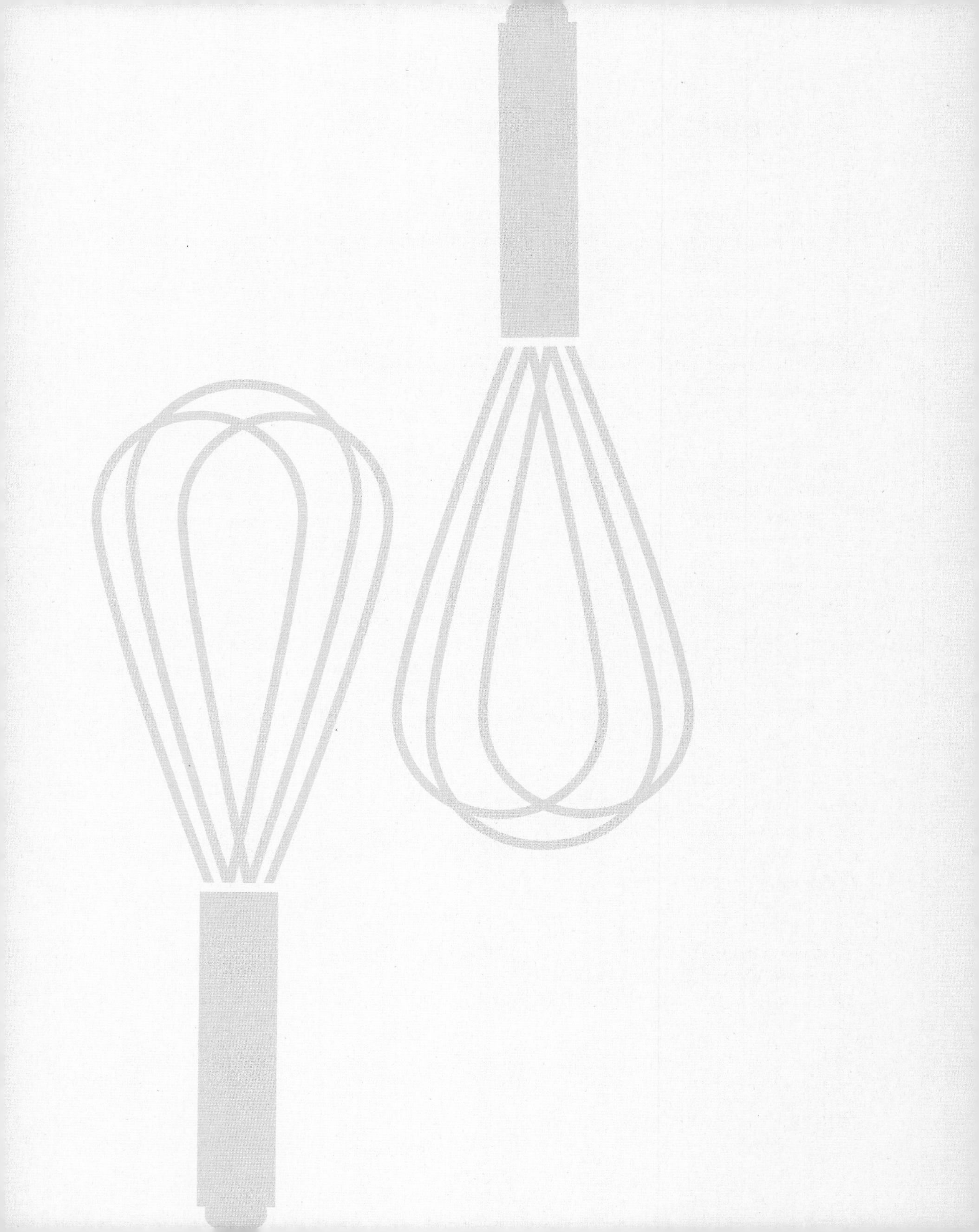

Napa Cabbage and Julienned Cucumber Quick Slaw

MAKES ABOUT 4 CUPS

I remember when I first heard "julienne your cucumber": I thought to myself, "Who's Julianne?!" This bright, tangy slaw will add some freshness to your steamed rice.

1½ cups julienned cucumber
¼ cup julienned red onion
2 cups shredded napa cabbage
¼ cup rice vinegar
2 tablespoons sesame oil
1 tablespoon natural cane sugar
1 tablespoon minced jalapeño pepper
1 tablespoon sliced green onion
2 tablespoons peeled and minced fresh ginger
1 generous tablespoon chopped cilantro
1 teaspoon toasted sesame seeds
2 teaspoons sea salt

1. If you're wondering the same thing about Julianne, here is a quick step-by-step guide to the julienne technique: Take your cucumber (or whatever you are going to chop) and cut it into four sections. Cut each section lengthwise into ⅛-inch sticks. Stack the sticks together and cut lengthwise again; this creates thinner sticks called julienne. Continue to use this cutting technique with the remaining cucumber pieces. After you've finished with the cucumber, put your skills to practice and julienne the red onion. Slice your cabbage about a fat ⅛ inch thick.
2. Place all three in a salad bowl and dress with the rice vinegar, sesame oil, sugar, jalapeño, green onion, ginger, cilantro, sesame seeds, and salt. Toss to combine.

Hello Sunshine Quinoa Tabbouleh

MAKES 2 SERVINGS

I firmly believe good food is medicine, and I had a chance to test that out when I was on an intense raw cleanse. I knew good nourishing food would help stave off hunger, so I developed this recipe. The pineapple and pepper really set this tabbouleh apart from traditional quinoa recipes. This sunshine salad has many bright and exciting bursts of flavor and is now in my regular rotation.

COOK'S NOTE: When cooking the quinoa, make sure it still has a bit of a bite to it and doesn't get mushy.

1 cup red quinoa
2 cups of water
1 cup diced fresh pineapple (not canned!)
½ cup grape or cherry tomatoes, sliced
2–3 tablespoons very thinly sliced serrano pepper
2 tablespoons very thinly sliced red onion
¼ cup olive oil blend
2 tablespoons freshly squeezed lemon or lime juice
1 teaspoon sea salt

1. Wash and drain the quinoa. In a medium saucepan over high heat, bring the grain and water to a boil. Cover and reduce heat to a low simmer. Cook until all the liquid is completely evaporated; the quinoa grains should "pop" and have what appears to be a small tail.
2. While the quinoa is cooking, mix the pineapple, tomatoes, serrano pepper, red onion, olive oil, lemon juice, and salt in a bowl. Once the quinoa is cool, add it to the bowl and toss together. Serve the tabbouleh with kebabs or by itself.

Roasted Red Pepper Soup

MAKES 2 SERVINGS

This soup is so silky and flavorful. I really recommend roasting your peppers fresh rather than using canned or jarred peppers. Fresh peppers have more natural sweetness and add a smooth texture to the soup. It's an extra step, but you will not regret it.

4 red bell peppers
¼ cup avocado oil, plus more to coat peppers
1 tablespoon chopped fresh garlic, plus a couple of generous pinches, divided
1 cup diced yellow onion
1½ cups whole tomatoes
2 cups vegan chicken stock
½ cup Dill Dip (page 12)
1 teaspoon sea salt
½ teaspoon freshly ground black pepper
1 tablespoon plant butter (I like Country Crock)
Parmesan Herb Croutons (page 29) (optional)

1. Preheat the oven to 350°F.
2. Slice the bell peppers in half and remove the seeds. Rub them with the oil and several generous pinches of garlic. Lay the peppers on a baking sheet and roast for 20 minutes, until they start to blacken and char in places. Remove from the oven and allow to cool. Once cool, remove the skin (it will just peel right off).
3. Heat the oil in a soup pot over medium-high heat, and add the onion, garlic, and red peppers. Cook until the onion turns translucent and golden-brown; the garlic should turn golden-brown as well, in 3–5 minutes. Add the whole tomatoes and stock and cook for 20 minutes. Add the Dill Dip and season with salt and pepper.
4. Remove from the heat. Using an immersion blender or a high-speed blender, blend until smooth, adding the butter. Serve with croutons, if desired, or with your favorite sammie.

French Onion Soup with Herby Cheese Toast

MAKES 3 SERVINGS

I really appreciate classic recipes, and I love getting inspired by them to make plant-powered dishes. Add some power greens with this soup and toast, and you have a lovely meal good for any time of day.

¼ cup cooking oil (avocado, safflower, or canola)
2 large onions, julienned, or about 8 cups
2 teaspoons chopped fresh garlic
1 tablespoon dried oregano leaves
½ tablespoon dried thyme
½ teaspoon sea salt
½ teaspoon freshly ground black pepper
¾ cup red wine
6 cups water
¾ cup tamari
1 tablespoon vegan Worcestershire sauce
¼ cup plant butter (I like Country Crock)
Herby Cheese Toast (page 87)

1. In a large soup pot, place the oil and heat on medium high. Add the onions, garlic, oregano, thyme, salt, and pepper, and sauté until caramelized and nicely brown, for about 20 minutes. Add the red wine and cook for 3–5 minutes, to cook off the alcohol, then add the water, tamari, Worcestershire sauce, and butter. Simmer for another 5 minutes or so. Make the Herby Cheese Toast and serve.

Crockpot Louisiana-Style Gumbo

MAKES 4 SERVINGS

Gumbo is one of those dishes we hear so much about—it has such a big reputation! I hope I have done it justice here. This version has none of the meat but all the flavor and the key components of any good gumbo: celery, onions, and bell pepper. Make extra and store it in the freezer.

1 teaspoon Cajun or Creole seasoning
¼ cup plus 2 tablespoons canola oil, divided
2 sausage links, cut into ¼-inch slices (I like Beyond Sausage, Hot Italian)
¼ cup all-purpose flour
½ cup diced yellow onion
½ cup diced green bell pepper
½ cup diced celery
2 teaspoons minced fresh garlic
2 teaspoons freshly squeezed lemon juice, or 2 tablespoons vermouth
3 cups veggie or vegan chicken stock (page 27)
1 cup chopped tomato
½ teaspoon white pepper
½ teaspoon freshly ground black pepper
½ teaspoon cayenne pepper
2 teaspoons fresh thyme
1 teaspoon sea salt
½ teaspoon light-brown sugar
1 teaspoon vegan Worcestershire sauce
2 small bay leaves, or 1 large
1 cup frozen okra
1 tablespoon thinly sliced green onion, green part only
Fresh parsley, chopped, for garnish
4 cups cooked rice

1. In a soup pot on medium heat, heat the Cajun seasoning and ¼ cup of the oil. Add the sausage and cook until browned, for 4–6 minutes. Once the sausage is cooked, use a slotted spoon to remove it from the pot. Plate it and set aside.
2. To make the roux, in the same pot on medium high, add the remaining oil and all-purpose flour. Cook the oil and flour until the mixture resembles peanut butter, stirring frequently; be careful not to burn the roux. This can take from 6 to 10 minutes.
3. Add the onions, bell pepper, celery, and garlic. Stir until the vegetables are slightly soft, for about 5 minutes. Be very careful not to burn them. If you are using vermouth, add it here to deglaze the pot.
4. Stir in the stock, tomatoes, white pepper, black pepper, cayenne pepper, thyme, salt, brown sugar, Worcestershire sauce (if using lemon juice in place of vermouth, add here), bay leaves, and frozen okra. Stir in the reserved sausage.
5. Using a wooden spatula, scrape the bottom of the pot to make sure there are no burnt bits stuck to the bottom. Put a lid on the pot and let your gumbo stew for 15–20 minutes.
6. Once the gumbo is done and the veggies are nice and tender, remove the lid and sprinkle the gumbo with green onions and parsley. Stir and serve the gumbo over the rice (I like jasmine rice with this).

Roasted Mushroom Bisque with Herby Cheese Toast

MAKES 3 SERVINGS

The Pacific Northwest is mushroom heaven. What better way to highlight those mushrooms than with a rich, silky bisque? The rich mushroom flavor really shines through this soup, complemented with fresh herbs and Dill Dip. The toast, though . . . the cheesy toast with the rich creamy soup really makes all the flavors come together for a perfect Northwest (or anywhere) light lunch.

¼ cup avocado oil
1 pound cremini or wild mushrooms, chopped
1 cup diced yellow onion
3 teaspoons fresh thyme
2 teaspoons chopped fresh garlic
½ teaspoon sea salt
½ teaspoon freshly ground black pepper
3 cups vegan chicken stock
1 cup Dill Dip (page 12)

1. Heat a soup pot to medium high with avocado oil. Add the mushrooms and onions; sauté for 15 minutes, or until the onion is nicely golden-brown and translucent. Season with the thyme, garlic, salt, and pepper, and cook for another 5 minutes. Add the stock and Dill Dip and remove from the heat. Using an immersion blender or a high-speed blender, blend the soup in batches until smooth. Serve with Herby Cheese Toast and fresh herbs.

Herby Cheese Toast

MAKES 1 BAGUETTE

While I suggest serving this toast with soup, I have to say that you will find yourself eating it by itself, no soup required.

¼ cup plant butter, room temperature (I like Country Crock)
¼ cup Dill Dip (page 12) or plain vegan mayonnaise
2 tablespoons vegan Colby Jack cheese shreds or whatever you like
½ teaspoon garlic (optional)
Pinch of fresh thyme
1 medium-size baguette

1. In a small mixing bowl, place the butter, Dill Dip, cheese shreds, garlic (if using), and thyme. Mix until well combined. Slice baguette in half, and then halve each piece lengthwise. Spread the butter mixture on the four baguette slices and put them under the broiler for 3–5 minutes, or until the cheese is golden-brown and bubbly.

Cauliflower and Yam Bisque

MAKES 2 SERVINGS

There's cauliflower soup . . . and then there's *this* cauliflower soup. The yam really adds a creamy sweetness to balance out the turmeric. The second time I cooked as executive chef at the Beard House, during the James Beard Foundation's vegan series, I made this soup as part of a six-course dinner. You can blend this soup and serve it with a fancy cilantro garnish, like we did at the Beard House. Or you can choose not to blend it; in which case, you should use less stock. Either way you win: it is full of endless flavor.

1 cup diced yellow onion
1 tablespoon minced fresh garlic
1 tablespoon peeled and grated fresh ginger
1 cup diced carrots
4 cups small cauliflower florets
2 cups diced sweet potato
5 cups veggie or vegan chicken stock, divided, plus more if needed (page 27)
2 teaspoons turmeric
1½ cups canned coconut milk
1½ teaspoons sea salt
½ teaspoon freshly ground black pepper
2 teaspoons freshly squeezed lemon or lime juice
Fresh cilantro, for garnish (optional)

1. In a soup pot over medium heat, simmer the onion, garlic, ginger, carrot, cauliflower, and sweet potato in ¼ cup of the vegetable stock until the vegetables are fragrant and starting to soften, for about 10 minutes. Add a splash more broth if the vegetables start to stick.
2. Add the turmeric; stir and cook for another minute.
3. Add the rest of the vegetable stock and simmer lightly until the cauliflower and sweet potato are tender, for about 20 minutes.
4. Stir in the coconut milk and, if needed, more vegetable broth to reach desired consistency.
5. Blend about one-half to three-quarters of the soup so it's somewhat creamy but still has some cauliflower and sweet potato chunks. You can do this by scooping it into a blender or by using an immersion blender right in the pot. If you prefer a completely creamy soup, feel free to blend it all until smooth.
6. Season with salt and pepper and a squeeze of fresh lemon juice.
7. Serve on its own or topped with fresh cilantro, if desired.

Blackened Tofu Grinders

MAKES 4 GRINDERS

I learned a lot about butter and spice as I toured the American South with Stevie Wonder. I would talk to all the chefs I could at hotels where we stayed. I always asked everyone what they were doing, and the chefs I met on the road were so incredible. They would share stories and dishes and tips. As I watched how they cooked, my curiosity about butter and spice grew. If you take your time preparing the tofu, this grinder won't disappoint. The tofu is nicely flavored, and the traditional grinder salad with Papa's Sammie Sauce really land the taste of this sandwich nicely.

COOK'S NOTE: Ideally, you'll want to marinate the tofu overnight; if you are short on time, make sure it marinates for at least 6 hours.

FOR THE BLACKENED TOFU GRINDERS

12 pieces Pan-Fried Cajun Butter Blackened Tofu (page 105)
1 tomato, sliced into about 12 thin slices
1 ciabatta baguette (I like Trader Joe's, or use any baguette 24 inches or so long)
Papa's Sammie Sauce (page 13)

FOR THE GRINDER SALAD

½ cup Papa's Sammie Sauce (page 13)
3 tablespoons hot vinegar from your Pepper Pot Pickled Onions (page 25)
2 tablespoons avocado oil
¼ teaspoon sea salt
¼ teaspoon freshly ground black pepper
Pinch of chili flakes
¼ cup very thinly sliced purple onion (or use Pepper Pot Pickled Onions, page 25)
2 cups thinly sliced iceberg lettuce

1. Cook the tofu according to the recipe on page 105.
2. While the tofu is cooking, slice the tomato and toast your baguette in a medium oven (350°F) for 2–3 minutes, or according to the package directions.
3. While the bread is toasting, make your grinder salad: in a small mixing bowl, combine the sammie sauce along with the rest of the ingredients, including the onions and lettuce. Set aside.
4. Once everything is ready, assemble your grinder by slicing the bread in half and adding Papa's Sammie Sauce to the bottom, as much as you like. Layer the pan-fried tofu along the length of the baguette and top with the tomatoes and the grinder salad. Put the top on the sub and cut into as many pieces as you like.

Bacon and Egg Grinder

MAKES 4 SANDWICHES

If your kind of people are sandwich lovers, this grinder will go over well. It is packed with flavor and texture. The sun-dried tomato relish really shines here and complements the smoky tofu and egg.

1 medium-size baguette or ciabatta (I like Trader Joe's)
1 pound Baba's Mesquite Smoked Tofu
Cooking oil for sautéing (avocado, safflower, or canola)
1 cup JUST Egg
Sun-dried Tomato Sammie Relish (page 20)
Papa's Sammie Sauce (page 13)
2 cups shredded romaine
Sprinkle sea salt
Sprinkle freshly ground black pepper

1. Toast the baguette according to the package directions, or if you have purchased a fresh loaf, slice and warm in a medium oven (350°F) for about 5 minutes.
2. Slice the tofu thin, like bacon, into as many slices as you can. Heat a medium skillet or pan to medium high and put in a couple of tablespoons of cooking oil, or simply coat the bottom of the pan. Cook the sliced tofu until it is crispy, for 2–3 minutes, flipping once to crispen both sides. Remove from the pan and set aside.
3. Wipe the pan out with a paper towel, if you like (but I would use the flavored oil here), and put in another drizzle of oil and the JUST Egg. I like to scramble my JUST Egg according to the package directions (see Pan-Fried Eggs on page 63). Once cooked, remove the egg from the pan and set aside.
4. To build the sandwiches, slice the bread in half and spread the sammie relish on the bottom half and the sammie sauce on the top. Layer the tofu along the bottom, top with the egg and lettuce, and sprinkle with salt and pepper. Place the top on, cut into pieces, and enjoy!

Portobello Gyros

MAKES 4 GYROS

I love anything in a gyro bread. This recipe is especially flexible: you can use portobello mushrooms or oyster mushrooms, plant-based chicken or seitan . . . basically any protein or meaty veg that's hanging out in your fridge. The bold Middle Eastern spices and the cool yogurt sauce coupled with all the fresh veggies make for a satisfying sandwich, no matter what veg or protein you choose.

1 pound portobellos plus stems or any mushrooms you like or plant-based meat
Gyro Spice Blend (page 28)
Avocado oil for cooking
4 pita breads
1 cup shredded lettuce
¼ cup thinly sliced onion
½ cup diced tomatoes
½ cup or more Yogurt Tahini Sauce (page 15)

1. If you are using portobellos, slice or chop them to your liking, making sure that all the pieces are a similar size; you can pull the stems off and use them as well. Sprinkle the pieces with a generous amount of gyro spice and set aside.
2. Heat a pan with cooking oil over medium-high heat. Sauté the portobello pieces until fragrant and starting to brown, for 1–2 minutes. Remove from the pan and keep warm.
3. To assemble the gyros, layer the portobello pieces on the bottom of the pitas, followed by the lettuce, onion, tomatoes, and yogurt sauce. Enjoy!

Tofu Bacon, Lettuce, and Tomato Sammie

MAKES 4 SANDWICHES

I made a version of this sammie as a club sandwich for my dad when he and my mom came to North Carolina to visit me while I was on the road with the *Songs in the Key of Life* tour. I made yam fries for my dad's sandwich, and he loved it. We serve this sammie with fries in the restaurant, and it is definitely a top seller. I am using deliciously sweet, tangy BBQ beans with this one. Try this combo: your taste buds will be electrified! It will have you emphatically saying, "That is gooooood."

Cooking oil for frying (avocado, safflower, or canola)
1 pound Baba's Mesquite Smoked Tofu, sliced thin like bacon
8 slices sandwich bread
Papa's Sammie Sauce (page 13)
Iceberg lettuce
1 extra-large heirloom or regular tomato, sliced
Tangy Skillet BBQ Beans (page 36)

1. Heat a medium skillet over medium-high heat and add a tablespoon or more of cooking oil. Add the tofu slices and fry until crispy, like bacon, for a minute or so on each side. Remove from the skillet.
2. While the tofu is frying, toast the bread slices. Build sandwiches by spreading the sammie sauce on each slice of bread (yep, bottom and top). Start with a generous amount of a soft crisp lettuce like iceberg; if you like a veggie-packed sandwich, add 2 slices of tomato. Top with 4–6 pieces of pan-fried tofu and put on the top slice of bread. Serve with BBQ beans and enjoy!

Everyday Suppers

Oftentimes, folks who have gone plant-based believe they have fewer options for suppertime. Well, that is about to change! My intention for this section is to make it easier for you to become vegan by offering a variety of delicious supper options. I was raised eating nothing but vegetables, and my family believed if we can help each other take a step toward compassion in our diets we should. These recipes fill in the space between the burger and the grain bowl, with delicious classics like Eggplant Parmesan, Chipotle Plant Beef and Bean Tostadas, or the ever-crowd-pleasing Wild Mushroom Ragù with Parmesan Gnocchi. When I say "suppers," I mean the whole enchilada: you'll find full meals here, with main courses paired with salads and sides. But please use these as you like: make them as complete suppers or try the sides individually. Whatever you do, you are not going to leave the table hungry.

Wild Mushroom Ragù with Parmesan Gnocchi

MAKES 2 SERVINGS

Who says you have to be in front of the stove for hours to make a restaurant-worthy dinner? I say you mix homemade and store-bought and cut your time in half but not your flavor. This tasty Italian dish combines hearty, earthy mushrooms with store-bought gnocchi and savory Parmesan cheese. It's a mic-drop kinda dinner for sure.

¼ cup olive oil blend, divided
1 pound wild mushrooms, such as maitake or lobster
½ cup diced yellow onion
1 tablespoon chopped fresh garlic
¼ cup red wine
1 cup veggie or vegan chicken stock (page 27)
1 (15-ounce) can whole tomatoes in juice
1–2 bay leaves
1 teaspoon fresh rosemary
1 teaspoon fresh thyme
1 teaspoon natural cane sugar
1 teaspoon sea salt
½ teaspoon freshly ground black pepper
1 package potato gnocchi
½ cup grated vegan Parmesan cheese, plus more for garnish (I like Violife)
Fresh parsley, for garnish (optional)

1. Bring a pot of water with a little salt to a boil for the gnocchi.
2. Heat a pan with half the olive oil to medium-high heat. Add the mushrooms, onion, and garlic. Sauté until the vegetables are fragrant and starting to brown, for 3–4 minutes. Pour in the red wine and simmer for 1–2 minutes to allow the alcohol to cook off, and then add stock.
3. Crush the whole tomatoes in your hand or pulse them briefly in a blender, leaving some chunks for the sauce, and add to the wine and stock. Season with the bay leaves, rosemary, thyme, sugar, salt, and black pepper. Simmer for 8–10 minutes.
4. While the sauce is simmering, cook the gnocchi for 2 minutes and remove immediately from the water. Toss with the rest of the olive oil, Parmesan, and parsley.
5. Serve the gnocchi with mushroom ragù in plates or bowls, with lots of Parmesan. Garnish with parsley, if you like.

Eggplant Parmesan with Alfredo Rigatoni and Lemon Olive Oil Arugula

MAKES 3–4 SERVINGS

Eggplant Parm is one of those standard home-cooked hardy dishes. I remember eating some version of this when I was a kid. I decided to give it a bit of a restaurant flair with the rigatoni. Topped with lemony arugula, this rich, bright dish makes a really nice supper.

2 cups rigatoni
¼ cup plant butter (I like Country Crock Plant Butter with Olive Oil)
1 tablespoon fresh garlic
¾ cup plain, unsweetened plant milk
½ cup vegan provolone
½ cup grated vegan Parmesan cheese
½ teaspoon white pepper, or more if you like
Salt
1 cup marinara sauce (page 19)
2–3 tablespoons water or plain, unsweetened plant milk
1 cup vegan mozzarella or provolone
2 cups arugula
Squeeze of lemon juice
Drizzle of olive oil
1 medium-size eggplant, sliced a fat ⅛ inch thick
1 cup plant milk
1 cup Black Pepper Breading (page 16)
1 cup or more panko breadcrumbs
¼ cup grated vegan Parmesan cheese
Cooking oil

1. Cook the pasta according to the package directions (2 cups dry rigatoni should make about 4 cups of pasta).
2. Make the Alfredo sauce: In a deep pan or pot, place the butter and garlic; sauté until the garlic is just golden-brown. Add the milk, provolone, Parmesan, white pepper, and salt. Cover and turn heat to low until the cheese melts. Mix the cooked rigatoni with the sauce and set aside.
3. Prepare the marinara sauce and set aside.
4. In a small pot, combine the water with the mozzarella; heat until the cheese melts and set aside.
5. In a small salad bowl, place the greens, lemon juice, olive oil, and salt and pepper to taste. Set aside.
6. To prepare the eggplant, slice it just a little fatter than ⅛ inch, but no more than ¼ inch, thick. Set up three mixing bowls: one with milk, one with Black Pepper Breading, and one with panko and Parmesan. Working in batches, dredge the eggplant slices first in the Black Pepper Breading, then in the milk, and then in the panko mixture.
7. Cover a plate with a layer of paper towels and set aside. Over medium-high heat, heat a deep pan or pot with cooking oil about two-thirds full. Once the cooking oil is hot (shimmering but not smoking), carefully drop the breaded eggplant slices into the oil and fry until dark golden-brown. Remove from the oil and set on the paper towels.
8. To assemble the dinner, split the Alfredo rigatoni among four plates and top with the fried eggplant. Spoon a few tablespoons of marinara on top, followed by 1–2 tablespoons of the melted cheese. Top with lemony greens, and sprinkle with more Parmesan, if desired.

The New South

The American South is such a culturally rich place with legendary food. This is a traditional American southern meal with a little added heat from our neighbors south of the border. For me, there is nothing better than when flavor meets heat—and this supper fits the bill.

Pan-Fried Cajun Butter Blackened Tofu

MAKES 6 SERVINGS

1½ cups plant butter, room temperature
3 tablespoons chopped fresh thyme leaves
2 tablespoons plus 1 teaspoon paprika
2 tablespoons plus 1 teaspoon cumin
2 tablespoons plus 1 teaspoon garlic powder
2 tablespoons plus 1 teaspoon onion powder
2 teaspoons sea salt
1 teaspoon cayenne pepper
½ cup vegan Worcestershire sauce
4 tablespoons soy sauce or tamari
1 tablespoon freshly squeezed lemon juice
3 tablespoons plus 1 teaspoon chopped fresh cilantro
1 cup vegan cream
2 pounds firm tofu (I like House Foods Extra Firm Tofu or Hodo Organic Extra Firm Tofu)
Cooking oil

1. To make Cajun blacking butter, combine butter, thyme, paprika, cumin, garlic powder, onion powder, salt, and cayenne in a bowl. Using a fork or your hand, mix the ingredients until well combined. Add the Worcestershire sauce, soy sauce, lemon juice, cilantro, and cream. Mix all the ingredients until well combined. Set aside the blacking butter.
2. Open the tofu, drain any excess water (*do not* press your tofu), and lay the block on its side. Cut carefully lengthways into thickish slices, somewhere between a ¼ inch and ½ inch wide. Different blocks of tofu have different thicknesses, but with most packages you will get 4–5 slices.
3. Lay the tofu slices out in a standard baking dish and rub each piece generously with the Cajun blacking butter. Marinate the slices overnight or for at least 6 hours in the fridge.
4. Once the tofu has set for some time, the butter will solidify. Take the tofu out of the fridge and allow the butter rub to soften. Scrape excess butter from the tofu and set aside.
5. Heat a medium pan or skillet on medium heat with oil. Place the tofu in the pan and cook for 4–5 minutes per side, or until dark golden-brown. Once the tofu is done on the second side, add the excess butter back in and allow to blacken as much as you desire.

Simply Good Southern Mac and Cheese

MAKES 6 SERVINGS

This mac and cheese is an easy crowd-pleaser. It's mild and cheesy, great for dinner or as an addition to your little one's lunch box. I use Violife cheeses because the cheese flavor comes through nicely. Did I mention this one is cheesy?

1 cup Violife Colby Jack shreds
1 pack Violife Cheddar slices, cut into small pieces
5 slices Violife smoked provolone, cut into small pieces
¼ cup Violife cream cheese
1 cup plain, unsweetened plant milk (I like soy)
½ cup plant butter
½ teaspoon white pepper
1 teaspoon sea salt
1 teaspoon Cajun seasoning
¼ teaspoon garlic powder
1½ cups elbow macaroni
2 cups vegan cream or mayonnaise

1. Preheat oven to 350°F.
2. In a medium pot over medium-high heat, combine Colby, Cheddar, provolone, cream cheese, milk, and butter and heat the ingredients just enough to combine (the sauce should be lumpy). Season with the white pepper, salt, Cajun seasoning, and garlic powder. Remove the sauce from the heat—remember, you want it to be very lumpy. Chill the sauce until cool to the touch.
3. While the sauce is chilling, cook the macaroni according to the package directions. Once the sauce is cool to the touch, add the cream and mix until well combined; it should be a superthick sauce.
4. Then mix in the macaroni and transfer it to a baking dish. Top with more cheese and cover very tightly in foil. Bake for 30 minutes. Remove the covering and allow to crisp under the broiler for 2–3 minutes.

COOK'S NOTE: Once the baking pan is filled with the mac and cheese mixture, cover the baking dish in plastic wrap first and then completely wrap the dish with foil, including the bottom. Doing this will trap lots of heat inside and really melt the cheese.

Tossed Salad Greens with Avocado, Black Beans, and Fresh Coriander Vinaigrette

MAKES 6 SERVINGS

I love a good simple salad, and this one delivers! Avocado and black beans add a smooth richness to stand up to the heat of the onions. You can serve this alongside any meal that needs a little extra garnish.

1 small container power salad greens (spinach, mizuna, chard, kale)
1 avocado, diced
1 cup black beans, rinsed and drained
Pepper Pot Pickled Onions for topping, as many as you like (page 25)
Fresh Coriander Vinaigrette (page 26)

1. In a salad bowl, place the greens and top with avocado, black beans, and pepper pot onions. Dress with a few tablespoons of the Fresh Coriander Vinaigrette.

Family Kebab Night

MAKES 4–6 SERVINGS

There is something so delicious about kebabs. Maybe it's the effort you have to put into making them that makes them so savory. This trio of kebabs will not disappoint. They are meaty and veggie packed, and there is something for everyone. Now, you can always just make one of these and have a delicious dinner, but I suggest trying the whole trio. If you make all three, you will have a robust dinner. But if you need more food, I suggest serving the skewers with the Hello Sunshine Quinoa Tabbouleh (page 79), along with grilled pita bread and Yogurt Tahini Sauce (page 15). You'll need 12–14 skewers for each recipe, and if you're using wooden skewers, don't forget to soak them ahead of time so they won't burn on the grill.

Kofta Skewers

MAKES 12–14 SKEWERS

These are by far the meatiest of the bunch, and they are boldly savory with a nod to the traditional. These may take a bit more effort, but they are totally worth the work.

1 cup roughly chopped yellow onion
1 tablespoon roughly chopped fresh garlic
1 cup roughly chopped red bell pepper
1 small jalapeño pepper, seeds and ribs removed, roughly chopped
½ cup fresh cilantro leaves
2 pounds ground plant meat (I like Beyond)
¾ teaspoon ground cumin
Heaping ¼ teaspoon ground cinnamon
Heaping ¼ teaspoon ground cardamom
Heaping ¼ teaspoon ground cloves
1½ teaspoons sea salt
¼ teaspoon white pepper
Yogurt Tahini Sauce (page 15), for serving
Pita bread, for serving

1. Preheat the grill to medium-high heat (450–500°F). Soak 12–14 wooden skewers for 20–30 minutes. Line a baking tray with parchment paper and set aside.
2. Place the onion, garlic, bell pepper, jalapeño, and cilantro in a food processor. Pulse until the vegetables are finely minced but not puréed. Using a strainer, thin kitchen towel, or cheesecloth, squeeze as much liquid as possible from the veggies. If they are still wet, transfer the minced vegetables to a sieve and use a rubber spatula to press out as much liquid as possible.
3. Place the strained vegetable mixture in a medium bowl and add the plant meat, cumin, cinnamon, cardamom, cloves, salt, and white pepper. Using your hands, mash the mixture until evenly combined. Then refrigerate for 2–3 hours until the mixture is firmer.
4. Scoop a portion of the mixture and mold it on a wooden skewer. Make sure each kofta kebab is about 1 inch thick, with one very long kebab per skewer. Repeat the process until you run out of mixture and skewers. Lay the skewered kofta kebabs on the parchment-lined tray.

5. Soak a paper towel in vegetable oil, roll it up, and then using tongs, rub it along the cleaned and completely heated grill grates.
6. Place the kofta kebabs on the lightly oiled, heated gas grill. Grill on medium-high heat for 4 minutes on one side; turn over and grill for another 3–4 minutes.
7. Serve with Yogurt Tahini Sauce and pita bread.

BBQ Tofu and Grilled Pineapple Skewers

MAKES 12–14 SKEWERS

When I first made these, I *loved* how they turned out. If you tear your tofu just right, the organic shape it takes creates more texture, and different flavor notes form char on the grill. It's a nice way to prepare tofu—light and tasty.

1 pound extra-firm tofu (I like House Foods or Hodo)
1 cup chopped red onion
1 cup BBQ sauce (I like Stubbs Original, or use your favorite BBQ sauce)
2½ cups fresh pineapple chunks, or about ½ pineapple

1. Preheat the grill to high heat (450–500°F). Soak 12–14 wooden skewers for 20–30 minutes.
2. Tear the tofu into 1½-inch pieces. In a medium bowl, place the tofu and onion and pour the BBQ sauce over them. Set in the fridge and allow to marinate for 2–3 hours. Once the tofu is marinated, remove from the fridge and add the pineapple. Toss to coat the pineapple with BBQ sauce. If you want more BBQ flavor in your pineapple, allow the fruit to sit in the BBQ sauce mixture for about 30 minutes.
3. Arrange the tofu, pineapple, and onion chunks on the soaked skewers. Lightly brush the skewers with oil. Put them on a plate and set aside.
4. Soak a paper towel in vegetable oil, roll it up, and then using tongs, rub the towel on the heated grill grate. Place the skewers on the grill and cook for 4–5 minutes. Flip the skewers and cook for another 4–5 minutes. Brush BBQ sauce on top of the skewers and flip again. Cook for 1–2 minutes and brush more sauce on the other side. Flip once more and cook for 1–2 minutes.

Veggie and Sausage Kebabs

MAKES 12–14 SKEWERS

This third option for kebabs gives you the best of everything with its chunks of sausage, peppers, mushrooms, and onions. This marinade is herby and light, allowing all the natural flavors of the veggies to shine through.

3 bell peppers, or 1 bag of multicolored sweet peppers, cut in 1-inch pieces (I like red, green, and orange)
½ large red onion, cut into 1-inch pieces
10 large baby bella (cremini) mushrooms, cut in half
1 package Impossible or Beyond sausage, cut into 1½-inch pieces
½ cup or more Fresh Herb Oil (page 20)

1. Preheat the grill to medium-high heat (450–500°F). Soak 12–14 wooden skewers for 20–30 minutes.
2. In a large bowl, place all the cut veggies and sausage. Add the herb oil and gently stir to combine everything. Arrange the veggies and sausage on the soaked skewers.
3. Soak a paper towel in vegetable oil, roll it up, and then using tongs, rub it along the cleaned and completely heated grill grates. Place the skewers on the grill and close the cover. Cook for 3–4 minutes, and then flip and cook on the other side for another 3–4 minutes, or until veggies and sausage are lightly charred.

Chicken Pasta Bake with Simple Bag Salad and Dressing

MAKES 4–6 SERVINGS

There is a confidence in uncomplicated food, and this dish was a part of my learning new ways to cook. It's also Stevie's kind of food—uncomplicated, homemade, just good. And hey, who doesn't love pasta, cheese, and tomato sauce?

COOK'S NOTE: I like to use Blackbird Original Seitan in this recipe because it lets all the other flavors in this dish come through, or you can find fresh seitan in your local Asian markets. If you are gluten-free, use oyster mushrooms or Daring Plant Chicken Pieces and gluten-free pasta. For the salad, grab your favorite prewashed greens mixture and add a chopped tomato. It really can be that simple.

3 cups penne
1 tablespoon olive oil
2 tablespoons cooking oil (avocado, safflower, or canola)
2 cups chopped seitan *or* oyster mushrooms, cut into ½-inch pieces
2 teaspoons chopped fresh garlic
½ cup Baba's Mesquite Smoked Tofu (optional)
2 cups chopped Roma tomatoes
2½ cups marinara sauce (page 19)
1 cup vegan mayonnaise or heavy cream
¼ cup grated vegan Parmesan cheese, divided (I like Follow Your Heart)
3 tablespoons chopped fresh parsley
2 cups whole baby spinach leaves
1¼ teaspoons sea salt
½ teaspoon freshly ground black pepper
1 cup shredded vegan mozzarella or Colby Jack cheese (I like Violife)
Salad greens
Dressing

1. Preheat the oven to 375–400°F.
2. Bring a pot with salted water and some oil to a boil for the penne pasta. Add the pasta and cook until al dente according to the package directions. Rinse and drain the pasta; toss with the oil and set aside.
3. Heat the cooking oil in a medium pot to medium high. Add the seitan and cook for 2 minutes until it starts to get tender. Add the garlic and cook until fragrant and slightly golden, for a minute or so.
4. Add the smoked tofu, if using, and the tomatoes, and cook for another 5 minutes, or until the tomatoes start to soften and break down into sauce. Add the marinara sauce and mayonnaise, half the Parmesan, parsley, spinach, salt, and pepper and fold into the pasta.
5. Transfer the pasta to a baking dish and top with the mozzarella. Cover the dish with plastic and foil, and bake in the oven until the cheese is melted and slightly bubbling on top, for about 15 minutes or so.
6. While the pasta bakes, put the salad greens in a serving bowl and set dressing on the side. Serve the baked pasta with the remainder of Parmesan.

COOK'S NOTE: Vegan cheese is very special. If the cheese is still not melted to your liking, remove the foil and plastic, turn your oven to broil, and set the dish back in for 5 minutes or so. That should do the trick. Remove from the oven and serve family style with a salad.

Something to Comfort Your Soul

The week my father died at home, we were on what could only be described as a death watch. For four impossibly long days, we waited with him for the time to come. The entire experience was almost indescribable as we quietly surrounded him and stood by, understanding the angels would be with us soon to take him home.

My father was a faith-filled, strong, courageous man. I always admired him, and ever since I was a little girl, I wanted to be like him. As I sat by my dad's bedside and waited with him, I remember asking him before he left where he was going, and he said emphatically, "To Heaven!" So I talked to him while we waited. While he was not able to talk to me the entire time, when he was able to talk, he told me the most amazing stories about his and my mother's love. He listened to my stories of crazy adventures and encouraged my wildest dreams, like he always did. He told me, "Thank you for taking care of me." He said everything would be OK and that he would see me soon. He told me like he always had, "Don't worry, I'm fine." He slipped into a coma shortly after that, and then we just waited in silence. My mom tried to get me to leave his bedside, but I refused. If you've experienced anything like this, you know you need to eat and how hard that is. My mother was in shock, doing all that she could to cook this meal for us, and it was a good, small comfort for our souls.

Slow Cooker Chick'n Noodle Soup

MAKES 2–3 SERVINGS

Chicken noodle soup smells like comfort to so many. This recipe uses tofu in the soup, though you can use Daring Plant Chicken Pieces (they have a great texture).

- 7 cups water, divided
- 3–4 packets chicken flavor soup mix, divided (I like Dragonfly Instant Artificial Chicken Flavor Broth)
- 1½–2 cups frozen tofu, thawed and torn into bite-size pieces
- Cooking oil for frying
- ¼ cup olive oil blend
- 1¼ cups chopped oyster mushrooms, in random-size chunks
- 1 cup diced yellow onion
- 1 tablespoon chopped fresh garlic
- ¼ cup dry porcini mushrooms
- ¾ cup diced carrots
- ¾ cup diced celery
- 1 tablespoon fresh thyme leaves
- 4 cups veggie stock
- 1 cup ditalini or rotelle
- Chopped fresh cilantro and scallions, for serving
- Lime or lemon slices, for garnish

1. In a medium saucepan, bring 3 cups of water to boil, then remove from the heat. Put in 2 packets of the soup mix and the raw tofu pieces. Marinate the tofu for about 2 hours; longer is always better. Remove the tofu from the marinade and squeeze out the excess liquid. Pan-fry in about 2 inches of cooking oil until crispy. Remove from the oil and set aside.
2. In a large soup pot, heat the olive oil on medium high; the oil should be slightly shimmering. Add the oyster mushrooms, onion, garlic, and porcini mushrooms, and cook until translucent and fragrant, about 5 minutes. Add the carrots and celery along with the pan-fried tofu and thyme leaves, and cook for another 5–7 minutes. Add the stock and 4 cups of water plus 1–2 packets of soup mix and the pasta. Bring everything to a boil and simmer for 5 more minutes until all the flavors get married.
3. Serve with the cilantro and a slice of lime.

COOK'S NOTE: Frying the tofu in about 2 inches of oil or more will add some fat to it and make your soup a little more authentic.

Warm Butter Biscuits

MAKES 12 BISCUITS

My dad would make southern-style biscuits without measuring a thing, and they were always perfect. Adding this biscuit recipe feels like an homage to him.

2 cups all-purpose flour
1 tablespoon granulated sugar
½ tablespoon baking powder
1 teaspoon sea salt
½ cup cubed very cold plant butter
½ cup plus 3 tablespoons cold oat milk
Melted plant butter for topping (optional)

1. Preheat the oven to 375°F. Line a baking sheet with parchment paper or spray with oil. Set aside.
2. In a large bowl, mix the flour, sugar, baking powder, and salt.
3. Add the cubed butter and coat with the flour. Using your hands, squeeze the butter pieces between your fingers, working the butter into the flour until the pieces turn sort of flaky and are a range of sizes. The batter should have a flaky look.
4. Pour the milk in, and using a soft spatula, fold the milk into the flour mixture until most of the flour is moistened but the dough is still crumbly. Form the dough into a ball. Don't overmix it, and don't worry about it being a perfect ball.
5. Turn the mixture out onto a floured work surface. With floured hands, pat the dough to a 1-inch-thick squarish shape. Fold the dough in half and cut it in half crosswise. Stack the two halves on top of each other, and press the dough into a rectangle again. Repeat 2–3 more times: folding, cutting, stacking, and pressing. This takes extra time, but it will work layers into your biscuits.
6. When you are finished rolling and pressing, roll the dough out to about 1 inch thick and cut either into squares or use a 2-inch cookie cutter for circles. There will be scraps if cutting into circles; gather the scraps to make one last biscuit. Place the biscuits on the baking sheet. For a better rise, freeze the biscuits for 20 minutes.
7. Bake for 18–20 minutes, or until the tops and bottoms are golden-brown. Remove from the oven and pour about 1 teaspoon of the melted butter over each if you like.

Garden Salad

MAKES 3 SERVINGS

I find when I am serving comfort food, a simple green salad on the side is a nice complement. This one is as simple as they come.

1 small head green leaf or romaine lettuce, cut into bite-size pieces (or 1 box prewashed mixed greens)
¼ small red onion, sliced
½–¾ carton cherry or grape tomatoes, sliced
1 small carrot, grated
Salad dressing (your favorite dressing or try Bacon Vinaigrette on page 22)

1. In a small salad bowl, place the salad greens, red onion, cherry tomatoes, and carrot. Dress with salad dressing and serve.

Spaghetti Ragù and Market Bread

MAKES 4 SERVINGS

What could be better than pasta and bread?

- 1 package spaghetti
- 3 teaspoons olive oil
- 3 teaspoons unsalted plant butter plus more for baguette
- 1 medium yellow onion, minced
- 2 cloves garlic, minced
- 1 pint cherry tomatoes, sliced
- 1 pound ground plant meat
- Kosher salt
- Black pepper, freshly ground
- 1 (28-ounce) can tomato sauce
- 1 baguette
- Fresh herbs

1. Add water and salt to a large pot of water and bring it to a boil. Place the spaghetti noodles in the boiling water and let them cook according to the package directions.
2. Heat another large pot over medium-high heat, and swirl in the olive oil and butter to evenly coat. Add the onion and garlic and cook, stirring frequently until softened and starting to caramelize, for about 5 minutes. Add the cherry tomatoes and cook until they are soft, for 2–3 minutes.
3. Add the plant meat and cook, stirring to break up the meat, for 10 minutes. Season with salt and pepper to taste.
4. Pour in the tomato sauce, lower the heat to medium, and cook the sauce, stirring, until slightly reduced, for 6–8 minutes.
5. If your baguette requires heating, place in the oven and cook according to the package directions. When warm, remove from the oven, slice, and slather generously with butter.
6. Divide the pasta between bowls, top with the ragù and the herbs, and serve with baguette slices.

Chipotle Plant Beef and Bean Tostadas

MAKES 4–6 TOSTADAS

I think the tostada is the most underrated version of the tortilla. I am elevating the forgotten one with this yummy, slightly spicy, meaty, crunchy dinner. Having a party or happy hour? Make mini tortillas to feed the whole gang.

COOK'S NOTE: The hot pickled onions need to sit for 4–6 hours, so plan ahead!

FOR THE CHIPOTLE BEEF

¼ cup cooking oil (avocado, safflower, or canola)
1 pound ground plant beef (I like Impossible)
½ cup minced onion
1 tablespoon chopped fresh garlic
2 tablespoons minced chipotle pepper in adobo sauce
¾ teaspoon sea salt
1 teaspoon ground cumin
1 teaspoon dried oregano
¼ cup tomato sauce
½ cup veggie or vegan chicken stock (page 27)
2 (16-ounce) cans vegan refried beans (I like Rosarita)
1 teaspoon Taco Seasoning (page 17)

FOR THE TOSTADA FIXIN'S

12 store-bought tostada shells
1 cup or more shredded lettuce (romaine or iceberg)
1 cup diced tomato
1 cup diced onion
1–2 avocados, diced
½ cup Jalapeño Dip (page 12)
Pepper Pot Pickled Onions (page 25, optional)
½ cup grated vegan Parmesan cheese (I like Follow Your Heart or Go Veggie)
½ cup shredded cilantro
Lime wedges, for serving

1. Heat a skillet or medium pan with cooking oil to medium high and add the plant beef, onion, garlic, and chipotle pepper. Sauté until the plant meat until it starts to brown and firm up, for about 7 minutes. Season with salt, cumin, and oregano, and stir in tomato sauce and veggie stock. Cook for 2–3 more minutes until the flavors are well combined. Scoop the plant beef out of the pan with a slotted spoon to leave oil behind for the refried beans.
2. Add the refried beans (I like black beans) and the taco seasoning to the same pan you cooked the plant beef in. Heat on medium for 2–3 minutes until warm.

MAKE ME A TOSTADA ALREADY!

1. Spread 2–3 tablespoons of refried beans on one tostada shell, top with the seasoned plant beef, and add the lettuce, tomato, onion, and avocado. Repeat with the remaining tostadas. Drizzle them generously with Jalapeño Dip and top with the spicy pickled onions and grated Parmesan. For a finishing touch, sprinkle with the cilantro. Serve with lime wedges.

Fresh Cilantro Pesto Pasta with Curry Tomato Salad and Pimiento Cheese Toast

MAKES 3–4 SERVINGS

I made this dish for Stevie while on tour, and it was an instant favorite. The fresh cilantro and mint in the pesto and the delicate curry flavor work deliciously with the richness of the cheese toast. This is a very modern and unexpected combo—and very good!

2½ cups rigatoni
1 cup Fresh Cilantro Pesto (page 15)
½ cup vegan sour cream (I like Follow Your Heart)
½ cup grated vegan Parmesan cheese, for topping

FOR THE TOMATO SALAD

½ pint multicolored cherry or grape tomatoes, sliced
2–3 green onions, sliced
1 jalapeño or serrano pepper, sliced (optional)
Juice of ½ lemon
1 tablespoon avocado oil
Generous pinch of curry powder
Flaky salt and black pepper

FOR THE PIMIENTO CHEESE TOAST

3–4 slices of toasted bread
Pimiento Cheese (page 31)

1. Cook the rigatoni according to the package directions with doneness to your liking (2½ cups of dry rigatoni should make about 5 cups of pasta). Set aside.
2. To make the tomato salad: Place the tomatoes in a small mixing bowl along with the green onion and jalapeño, if using. Squeeze ½ lemon or more if you like, drizzle with the avocado oil, and add curry powder, and salt and black pepper. Gently toss to combine and set aside.
3. Heat a saucepan over medium heat and put in the pesto and sour cream. Heat until **warm** and stir to combine. Reserve about 1 cup of pesto mixture: you will need ¾ to 1 cup of sauce for 5 cups of cooked pasta. Add the pasta and toss to completely coat.
4. To finish, split the pasta into serving dishes, top with a spoonful or two of tomato salad, and sprinkle generously with Parmesan. Serve with pimiento cheese toast.

Creole Tempeh with Wilted Collards and Jasmine Rice

MAKES 2–3 SERVINGS

This is a date-night-at-home kind of dinner. Tempeh is tofu's hipper, cooler, younger sister and has a nutty flavor all her own, and she soaks up marinade really nicely. This is fancy enough as it is, but you can make it a little bit fancier with celery root puree instead of rice—and maybe a Bordeaux. This one is for the grown-ups.

COOK'S NOTE: You'll want to marinate the tempeh for at least 6 hours or overnight, so plan accordingly!

1 cup white wine
⅓ cup olive oil
1½ tablespoons tamari
1 Roma tomato, chopped, then smashed
¼ cup whole tomatoes in juice, crushed (use your hand to smash the tomatoes)
1 small shallot, sliced
1 tablespoon fresh thyme leaves
1 tablespoon chopped fresh parsley
½ teaspoon dried thyme
¼ teaspoon cayenne pepper
1 teaspoon paprika
½ teaspoon sea salt
½ teaspoon white pepper
½ teaspoon dried oregano leaves
½ teaspoon lemon zest
¼ teaspoon sugar
1 (8-ounce) package unflavored tempeh (I like Turtle Island)
1–2 tablespoons cooking oil (safflower or avocado)
1 tablespoon plant butter

1. In a bowl, place wine, olive oil, tamari, Roma tomato, plus whole tomatoes in juice. Add the shallot and season with fresh thyme, parsley, dried thyme, cayenne pepper, paprika, sea salt, white pepper, oregano leaves, lemon zest, and sugar. Mix all the ingredients and set aside.
2. Remove the tempeh from the package and cut into 3 even pieces and then cut in half to about ¼ inch thickness: don't use thick tempeh. Spread half the marinade on the bottom of a small baking dish, add the tempeh on top, and pour the remaining marinade over the tempeh. Let set for 6–8 hours or overnight.
3. Once the tempeh is marinated, heat a sauté pan over medium-high heat with a thin coating of cooking oil. Pan-fry the tempeh until golden-brown on each side. Take about a half cup of leftover marinade, and in a separate sauté pan, heat and allow the wine to cook off for 3–5 minutes. Add the butter, turn the heat off, and stir.
4. Split the rice between plates, and top with the tempeh and 2 tablespoons or more of the sauce. Serve with the wilted collards salad.

Wilted Collards

MAKES 3 SERVINGS

Kale's been having its moment, but did you know that collard greens are even more nutritious *and* tasty? The mild, slightly sweet cashew rub is perfect for the tough sharpness of collards or yes, that other green, the nutty earthiness of kale.

2 cups raw cashews
½ cup water
1 tablespoon nutritional yeast
2 teaspoons porcini powder
2 teaspoons olive oil
1 teaspoon sea salt
¼ teaspoon freshly ground black pepper
1 bunch fresh collards

1. In a blender, place the cashews, water, nutritional yeast, porcini powder, olive oil, salt, and pepper. Blend until very smooth; taste and adjust salt, if needed. (If you have any leftover cashew rub, store it in a mason jar. It will keep for 5–7 days in the fridge.)

2. Trim and discard the bottom stems of the collard greens. Stack the leaves and roll them up. Cut the roll into slices, about a fat ⅛ inch thick, and put them in a bowl. Pour a generous ¼ cup of the rub onto the collards and rub it into them. Add more if the slices look dry. Set aside and allow the collard greens to wilt, for about 15 minutes.

Jasmine Rice

MAKES 2 CUPS

1 cup jasmine rice
1 cup water
Pinch of sea salt

1. Rinse the rice through a strainer. In a small saucepot over medium-high heat, bring the rice and water to a boil. Reduce the heat to very low and cook until the water is absorbed, for about 12 minutes. Fluff and serve with the salt, tempeh, and greens.

Creamy Chipotle and Fresh Tomato Spaghetti with Grilled Zucchini and Roasted Yams

MAKES 4 SERVINGS

This is such a fun and summery twist on traditional spaghetti. The chipotle gives the pasta an unexpected, slightly spicy kick, and the grilled and roasted veggies add variety to the plate and are super yummy for everyone.

FOR THE PASTA

1 teaspoon sea salt
1 cup sliced onion
4 garlic cloves, separated
2 bay leaves
1 teaspoon olive oil
3 tablespoons plant butter
2 teaspoons vegan chicken flavor
½ pound spaghetti

FOR THE CHIPOTLE PASTA SAUCE

5 Roma tomatoes
½ teaspoon Mexican oregano
1–2 chipotle peppers in adobo sauce
½ cup vegan cream
¼ cup Jalapeño Dip (page 12)
⅔ cup pasta water
¼ cup grated vegan Parmesan cheese
1½–2 teaspoons natural cane sugar
1 teaspoon sea salt
2 tablespoons plant butter
¼ cup minced onion
1 tablespoon chopped cilantro

FOR THE GRILLED ZUCCHINI

Wedged Roasted Yams (page 24)
1–2 fresh zucchinis, sliced lengthwise into 4–6 pieces, depending on size
Olive oil for rubbing
Salt and pepper
Fresh herbs

1. Fill a pot with water and add the salt, onion, garlic, bay leaves, olive oil, butter, and vegan chicken flavoring. Bring to a boil and add the spaghetti. Reduce the heat to a simmer and cook until the pasta is al dente or to your liking.
2. Bring a separate pot of water to a boil and add the tomatoes until the skins pop. Remove the tomatoes from the water and put in a blender, along with the oregano, chipotle peppers, cream, Jalapeño Dip, pasta water, Parmesan, sugar, and salt. Blend all the ingredients until very smooth.
3. Heat the butter in a separate large saucepan. Add the onions and sauté until translucent and slightly golden-brown. Then pour in the sauce and add the spaghetti. Simmer for 3–4 minutes to combine flavors; the pasta should be on the drier side. Serve sprinkled with a generous amount of Parmesan and garnished with fresh cilantro. Serve family style in the same cooking pan if you like.

PREPARE THE VEGGIES

1. Cook the yams according to the recipe. Rub all sides of the zucchini slices with olive oil and season with salt and pepper and your choice of fresh herbs. Grill the zucchini on a grill or in a sauté pan on medium high, for about 2 minutes a side, turning once. Serve family style on a tray or plate up for dinner.

Sriracha Meatloaf with Steamed Rice and Sautéed Baby Bok Choy

MAKES 4–6 SERVINGS

What can I say about meatloaf? It is a quintessential American dish that many of us have strong feelings about: some of us aren't sure if we really like it (and some of us proudly love it!). We had tofu versions of meatloaf growing up and that is my go-to. But with the invention of plant meat, I thought *why not give it a new innovative spin?* Inspired by yummy Asian flavors, comforting rice, and the always underappreciated bok choy, I think this combination really does a baked loaf of meat justice.

1 pound Impossible meat, thawed
1½ teaspoons chopped fresh garlic
1½ teaspoons chopped fresh ginger
2 tablespoons green onion
2 tablespoons chopped fresh cilantro
1½ tablespoons sriracha
1 tablespoon sesame oil
½ teaspoon black pepper
2 tablespoons ketchup
Cooking spray

FOR THE MEATLOAF TOPPING

¼ cup ketchup
1 tablespoon sriracha
1 tablespoon cilantro
½ teaspoon sesame seeds

FOR THE STEAMED RICE

2 cups jasmine rice

FOR THE SAUTÉED BABY BOK CHOY

½ pound baby bok choy, sliced in half lengthwise
1–2 tablespoons avocado oil
Salt

1. For the meatloaf, preheat the oven to 350°F.
2. Place the Impossible meat in a mixing bowl and add the garlic, ginger, green onion, cilantro, sriracha, sesame oil, black pepper, and ketchup. Using your hands or a sturdy spoon, mix all the ingredients well. Spray a loaf pan with cooking spray, press the meatloaf mixture into the pan, and top with the meatloaf topping. Cover with foil and cook for 35 minutes and then uncovered for an additional 15–20 minutes. This meatloaf is better the next day, so put it in the fridge; it will firm up nicely and you can slice it into about 1-inch slices, then serve with the steamed rice and sautéed bok choy.
3. For the steamed rice, cook the rice according to the package directions.
4. For the baby bok choy, in a pan, heat the avocado oil on medium high until it is shimmering. When the oil is hot, place the bok choy cut-side down in the pan; the bok choy should sizzle when it hits the pan. Cook the bok choy until it is nicely charred on the flat side, for 1–2 minutes; then add 2–3 tablespoons of water to the pan to steam the bok choy, for 1 minute or so. Sprinkle with salt and serve.

COOK'S NOTE: *For Beyond meat, cook 40 minutes covered and then 15 minutes uncovered.*

St. Regis
China

BBQ Tofu Steaks with Wedged Roasted Yams

MAKES 3 SERVINGS

Along with "Where do you get your protein?" one of the most common comments about plant-based eating is to malign tofu. So this recipe is for anyone who thinks tofu is flavorless. This modern "meat" and potatoes dish is beyond flavorful and a fun twist on classic BBQ and yams. So like I tell all my friends, "Don't be afraid of the tofu."

COOK'S NOTE: This recipe calls for a marinating time of 24–48 hours, so plan ahead.

FOR THE BBQ TOFU STEAKS

1 pound of extra-firm tofu
½ plus ¼ cup avocado oil or olive oil
½ cup loosely packed brown sugar
½ cup tamari or soy sauce
½ cup vegan Worcestershire sauce
2 tablespoons apple cider vinegar
2 tablespoons chopped fresh garlic
4 teaspoons chili powder
4 teaspoons ground cumin
2 teaspoons paprika
½ teaspoon liquid smoke (I use Stubb's mesquite)
¼ teaspoon cayenne pepper
¼ teaspoon black pepper

FOR THE WEDGED ROASTED YAMS

1½–2 pounds white-flesh yams (1–2, depending on size)
¼ cup herb oil (page 20), olive oil, or avocado oil
½ teaspoon salt
¼ teaspoon pepper
2 tablespoons vegan Parmesan, divided
2 teaspoons fresh garlic
Fresh cilantro, for garnish
Green onion, for garnish

1. Remove the tofu from package and slice it into six "steaks," about 2 inches long by ⅜ inches thick. Set aside.
2. To make the marinade, in a small bowl place ½ cup of the avocado oil, brown sugar, tamari, Worcestershire sauce, apple cider vinegar, garlic, chili powder, cumin, paprika, liquid smoke, cayenne, and black pepper. Mix all the ingredients until well combined. Pour a layer of marinade in the bottom of a flat dish, layer the tofu on top of the marinade, and pour the remaining marinade over the tofu to cover. Marinate for 24–48 hours.
3. When ready to cook, heat a pan with about 1/4 cup of the avocado oil to medium heat. Lay the tofu cutlets in the pan and cover with a lid. The sugar in the marinade will burn easily, so keep on a medium-low heat and allow the tofu to cook internally for about 7 minutes per side. Once fully cooked, turn up the heat just long enough to crispen and brown the outside of the tofu.
4. For the yams, preheat the oven to 350°F. Cut the yams in half crosswise. If the yams are really large, cut them in half lengthwise and into about ¾-inch wedges for 4–6 wedges per half. Smaller yams will yield 3–4 wedges per half. Place the yams in a bowl and toss with the herb oil, salt, pepper, Parmesan, and garlic until well coated. Transfer the yams to a baking sheet cut-side down. Cover with foil and cook for 20 minutes and then uncovered for an additional 15 minutes. Serve with the BBQ Tofu Steaks.

Macho Burritos

MAKES 4 BURRITOS

There is nothing like a good burrito: I can't remember exactly why we call this the macho burrito at Plum Bistro, but I do know we have patrons that come every day just for this burrito. The beans and rice are so comforting, while the cheese and avocado add texture and more flavor. The flavor king in all this is Baba's Chorizo Taco Mix—it really helps level up the burrito. If you can't find taco mix, use your favorite plant-based chorizo. Who knows: this may make its way into your daily routine as well.

Avocado oil for cooking
2 cups Baba's Chorizo Taco Mix
2 cups Papa's Black Beans (page 165)
2 cups Spanish Rice (page 24)
1 cup or more vegan Colby Jack cheese
4 extra-large spinach tortillas
4–8 tablespoons Chipotle Dip (page 13, optional)
4 tablespoons vegan sour cream (optional)
1 cup or more pico de gallo (page 25)
2 avocados, sliced
4 cups mixed spring greens, loosely packed

1. Heat a pan with avocado oil to medium high and add the chorizo, black beans, rice, and cheese; cover and allow to heat up to a simmer, until the cheese melts, for 2–4 minutes. Then remove from the heat.
2. Lay your tortillas out; if using, spread the Chipotle Dip and sour cream on each one. Split the bean mixture among the four tortillas, top with the pico de gallo, avocado, and spring mix; roll up and set aside.
3. Wipe any large chunks from your pan and put in a tad of cooking oil. Over medium heat, brown the burritos on all four sides, for 2–3 minutes per side, until just crispy. Remove and serve with extra chipotle.

My American Guy Cheeseburger

MAKES 4 BURGERS

I call this burger "my American guy" because I want every nonvegan dad who gets dragged to my restaurant by his teenage daughter who is no longer eating anything with a face to find something that speaks to him. I want him to understand his baby girl is not crazy for not eating animal-based meat and this vegan thing might be OK. These burgers are a classic interpretation of a good cheeseburger. It satisfies the burger craving and hits the spot—for skeptical dads and for everyone else.

COOK'S NOTE: Impossible is a favorite brand of mine, but I don't recommend it for this recipe; it will not stay together with all the added ingredients and is better suited for a different use.

1 pound ground plant beef (I like Before the Butcher Uncut Burger or Beyond Burger)
¼ cup minced yellow onion
1 tablespoon vegan Worcestershire sauce
½ tablespoon chopped fresh garlic
2 tablespoons chopped mushrooms
2 tablespoons burger seasoning (page 22)
1–2 tablespoons cooking oil (avocado, safflower, or canola)
4–8 slices vegan cheese (I like Daiya or Violife, or use your favorite sliced vegan cheese)
4 hamburger buns
½ cup or more Special Sauce (page 23)
4 good-size pieces of lettuce (butter, romaine, or iceberg)
1 large tomato, sliced
Bread and butter pickles
Sautéed onions (page 23)

1. In a mixing bowl, place the plant beef, onion, Worcestershire sauce, garlic, mushrooms, and burger seasoning. Mix the ingredients until well combined. Using a scoop or your hands, form four burger patties. Heat a pan on medium-high heat (or grill if grilling outside) and add the cooking oil. Place the patties in the pan and cook for 4–5 minutes per side. After the patties have been cooking on their second side for about 2 minutes, add the cheese slices. Cover the pan to allow the cheese to melt.
2. Allow everyone to assemble their own cheeseburgers, or take four perfectly soft burger buns, spread Special Sauce on the bottoms, add a piece of lettuce, then add the burger patties topped with cheese, tomatoes, pickles, and sautéed onion. Add more sauce to the top burger bun and secure with a burger pick. Serve with fries, chips, or salad and enjoy!

COOK'S NOTE: Add rich flavor and crispy texture to your burger buns by toasting them. To toast a bun on a grill, grill pan, or griddle, split the bun open, place it cut-side down on the grill, and grill until light golden-brown, for about 10 seconds.

Buffalo Portobello Burgers

MAKES 4 BURGERS

Here is a great new way of looking at burgers! The meaty, crispy portobello mushroom and the tangy hot sauce make the perfect mixture of texture and flavor on a bun. Add ranch to cool it down a bit. Perfection. You will want to make this multiple times a week—I'm sure of it.

- 2 cups plain, unsweetened plant milk (I like soy)
- 2 teaspoons cider vinegar
- 1 cup or more Black Pepper Breading (page 16)
- 1 cup or more Panko Breading (page 17)
- Cooking oil for frying (avocado, safflower, or canola)
- 4 medium-size portobellos
- 4 burger buns
- 1 cup or more Vegan Ranch (page 18)
- 1 cup mixed salad greens, loosely packed
- 1 cup or more Buffalo Sauce (page 18)
- ½ English cucumber, sliced
- Sautéed onions (page 23)

1. In a mixing bowl, place the plant milk and vinegar, give it a stir, and set aside. In another mixing bowl, place the Black Pepper Breading; in a third bowl, place the Panko Breading. Line a plate with paper towels and set aside.
2. Fill an 8-inch or larger pot two-thirds with cooking oil and heat over medium high until the oil starts to look thin, but is not smoking, for 4–5 minutes.
3. While the oil is heating, bread your portobellos. Start by dipping one portobello in the milk mixture, then dip it in the Black Pepper Breading. Dip it in the milk mixture again, and then into the Panko Breading. Set aside and repeat with all the mushrooms. Fry the portobellos in batches, depending on the size of your pot. Fry them until golden, for about 4 minutes, and then set them on the paper towel–lined plate.

SO JUST MAKE ME A BURGER!

1. This burger will benefit from a toasted bun. To toast a bun on a grill, grill pan, or griddle, split the bun open, place it cut-side down on the grill, and grill until light golden-brown, for about 10 seconds.
2. On the bun, spread some ranch and add a few mixed greens. Toss your portobello in Buffalo Sauce, place it on the bottom of the bun, and top with the cucumber and onions. Add more ranch and secure the top bun with a burger pick. Enjoy with fries, chips, or salad.

Creole Sloppy Joe

MAKES 6–8 BURGERS

Who doesn't love a sloppy joe? It's a deliciously messy meat and bread burger with ketchup that literally gives you permission to be, well, sloppy. This is a great recipe for plant meat like Beyond or Impossible—it really brings home that authentic sloppy joe flavor. Make it for your crew and see what they think!

Neutral oil for cooking (I like safflower oil)
1 cup minced yellow onion
1 cup minced green bell pepper
2 pounds ground plant meat (Beyond, Impossible, or your favorite plant ground beef)
1 teaspoon garlic powder
1 teaspoon sea salt
1 tablespoon Dijon mustard
2 tablespoons vegan Worcestershire sauce
2 tablespoons cider vinegar
2 tablespoons light-brown sugar
1 (14-ounce) can whole tomatoes, diced, with juice
½ cup ketchup
2 teaspoons Creole seasoning
Buns, for serving
Pickles, for serving (optional)
Chips, for serving

1. Heat a little cooking oil in a sauté pan and add the onion, bell pepper, and vegan beef. Cook over medium high until the meat is golden-brown and the vegetables are soft, for about 10 minutes. If the mixture is a little oily, drain the oil. Season with garlic powder, salt, mustard, Worcestershire sauce, cider vinegar, brown sugar, tomatoes plus their juice, ketchup, and Creole seasoning. Mix well and simmer for 5–7 minutes. Serve on soft hamburger buns with pickles, if desired, and chips.

Oyster Mushroom Po' Boys

MAKES 2 SANDWICHES

Oyster mushroom calamari (page 71)
¼ cup or more Tabasco Aioli (page 14)
Juice of ½ lemon
2 tablespoons olive or safflower oil
2 soft hoagie rolls
1 cup finely shredded romaine or iceberg lettuce
1 tomato, thinly sliced
Salt and pepper or seasoned salt (I like Lawry's or Johnny's)

1. Prepare the calamari according to recipe directions.
2. In a small mixing bowl, squeeze about half a lemon and add the oil. Mix and set aside.
3. To assemble the sandwiches, cut the rolls in half and toast, if desired. Spread some Tabasco Aioli on the inside of each roll on both sides. Toss the lettuce and tomato with lemon and oil, and season with salt and pepper. Layer the rolls with tomato slices and romaine lettuce, and fill with the fried mushrooms until slightly overflowing. Serve immediately while the oyster mushrooms are still warm.

GIANT

Life's Little Joys

My nephew is that kid who never meets anyone who is not a friend; according to him, "If we are the same size, then that's a friend." Consequently, my life is filled with beautiful bright kid energy. I cook a lot for my nephew and his friends, so this section is in honor of them. Kids today have such a voice in food, and we have a great opportunity for progress and change when we feed them. My belief is if we want to move toward a society that consumes less animal-based meat, we have to start with what we feed our children. In this section, you won't find too many meat replacements; rather, you will find a good foundation of grains, legumes, tofu, fruits, veggies, and some fun things like corn dogs, pizza pockets, grilled cheese, and ramen. It can be hard to get calories, proteins, veggies, and fiber into their little bodies, so my goal for these meals is to create variety for your little ones. It is possible for convenience, yumminess, and nutrition to work cooperatively for lunch boxes or anytime meals. And honestly—these recipes are good for the big kids too.

Pajamas and Pancakes Brunch Party!

MAKES 6–8 SERVINGS

This is a modern way to enjoy a plant-based brunch that works for everyone and for any special occasion. I created this for a sleepover party for my nephew. It's also great for a weekend playdate or a fun birthday party. However you prepare it, your kiddos will have a belly full of yummy food!

KIDDIE BRUNCH MENU

Strawberry Skillet Jam (page 30)
Coconut Cheesecake Butter (page 32)
Vegan chicken nuggets
Funfetti Pancakes (page 151)
Breakfast Sausage (page 60)
Skillet Breakfast Potatoes (page 59)
Pan-Fried Eggs (page 63)
1 pint blueberries
½ cantaloupe, cubed
1–2 bananas, sliced

1. You can prep the Strawberry Skillet Jam and Coconut Cheesecake Butter ahead of time.
2. Cook the chicken nuggets according to the package directions. Cook the Funfetti Pancakes according to the recipe and the breakfast sausage according to the package directions, or follow the recipe on page 60. Prepare the Skillet Breakfast Potatoes and Pan-Fried Eggs according to the recipes. For the fruit salad, combine the blueberries, cantaloupe, and bananas.

Funfetti Pancakes

MAKES 12 OR MORE COIN PANCAKES

Kids love these, but let's face it, adults do too. I include instructions for pancakes, but I won't stop you if you want to make waffles. Just follow the instructions for your waffle maker.

COOK'S NOTE: If you have sweetened or flavored oat milk, reduce the amount of sugar to taste. I use pretty sprinkles from the grocery story; try your favorites here.

2 cups plain, unsweetened oat milk (I like Chobani)
2 tablespoons cider vinegar
2 cups all-purpose flour
¼ cup natural cane sugar
2 tablespoons baking powder
1 teaspoon sea salt
2 teaspoons vanilla extract
1–2 tablespoons cooking oil (avocado, safflower, or canola)
2 tablespoons or more sprinkles, for garnish (optional)
Maple syrup, for serving

1. Pour the milk into a bowl, then add the vinegar and set aside.
2. In a large mixing bowl, place flour, sugar, baking powder, and salt. Mix to combine and set aside. The milk mixture, meanwhile, should have thickened up; add the vanilla extract and mix to combine.
3. Make a well in the pancake flour batter and pour the milk mixture into the flour. Fold the two together until just combined; don't overmix. Allow to set for just a few minutes.
4. Heat your skillet to medium heat and add the oil. When the oil is hot (drops of water will sizzle), add the batter in about 1-ounce scoops. Cook until the top of the pancake batter starts to bubble, for 1–2 minutes, depending on the pancake size. Flip and cook on the other side for another minute or so. Plate and serve with sprinkles, if desired, and maple syrup.

Mama's Golden Melon Milk

MAKES 2–3 GLASSES, DEPENDING ON GLASS SIZE

Our house is teeming with fresh fruit, and inevitably some of it gets super ripe. If you don't know what to do with your overripe melons, try this heart-healthy drink loaded with fiber, potassium, and vitamin C. This drink is best with fruits like cantaloupe, papaya, or mango at the peak of ripeness or try some just-ripe bananas when they are perfectly bright yellow. This is best with fresh fruit for an incredibly silky smooth, yummy drink. You can also pour it into popsicle molds for a refreshing treat for the whole family.

2 cups very ripe fresh or frozen cantaloupe
1 cup oat milk (add ½ cup more milk if using frozen fruit)
Pinch of sea salt
½ teaspoon vanilla extract
½–1 teaspoon agave (optional)

1. In a blender, place melon, milk, salt, vanilla extract, and agave (if using), and blend until smooth. Serve in glasses or pour into popsicle molds and freeze until firm.

Good Morning Good-Belly Strawberry Smoothie

MAKES 1 LARGE GLASS OR 2 SMALL GLASSES

Sometimes you ask your kid to eat, and they flat-out say no. This yummy, good-belly smoothie is just for those times. It's packed with fiber, omega-3 fatty acids, probiotics, vitamin C, and potassium, plus a little sweet tanginess from the strawberries and orange juice. This will have your little one and you, too, saying, yes, please!

1 cup frozen strawberries
1 medium banana
½ cup Plain Chia Pudding (page 33)
½ cup orange juice
1 cup almond milk
1 tablespoon agave (optional)

1. Place all the ingredients in a blender and blend until smooth.

You love
Puppy

Sausage and Egg Breakfast Burrito

MAKES 4 BIG BURRITOS OR 8 LITTLE ONES

These burritos are great when you have just a moment to sit down before the morning craziness or are running out the door to eat breakfast in the car. Who can say no to all their favorites wrapped up in one delicious package? We serve this at Plum, and we always run out; it is such a crowd-pleaser. The sausage, egg, and potato combination is hearty enough to keep you going throughout the morning. Throw in some avocado for a little extra richness and enjoy! Breakfast burrito? Yes, please.

Avocado oil for cooking, divided
1 pound Breakfast Sausage (page 60) or your favorite brand
1 cup or more shredded vegan Mexican cheese
4 cups frozen hash browns
1 cup JUST Egg
4 extra-large flour tortillas or 8 mini tortillas
1 cup pico de gallo (page 25)
Avocado slices, for serving

1. Heat a pan with oil to medium high. Form the sausage meat into four separate patties and cook on one side for 3 minutes, or until the patties start to brown and firm up. Flip the patties and break them up a bit, using the spatula; sprinkle the cheese on top. Allow to cook until the cheese melts and the bottoms firm up, for about 3 minutes. Remove from the heat and set aside.
2. Cook the hash browns according to the package directions, ensuring they are crispy, and set aside.
3. I like to scramble my JUST Egg according to the package directions (see Pan-Fried Eggs on page 63).
4. To assemble the burritos, divide the hash browns among the four tortillas, top with the sausage mixture, and then add egg. Top with pico de gallo, and roll or fold up the burritos.
5. Pour a tad of avocado oil in a nonstick pan and toast the burritos on all sides, for 1–2 minutes. Serve with avocado and more pico or hot sauce.

Yogurt Chia Pudding with Banana Bread and Breakfast Sausage

MAKES 2 SERVINGS

Sometimes breakfast for lunch makes you the cool kid! Fill your little one's belly with probiotics from the yogurt and large amounts of fiber and omega-3 fatty acids, plenty of high-quality protein, and several essential minerals and antioxidants from the chia and berries. Add yummy banana bread and sausage, and you will have a happy kid with a happy belly!

2 cups yogurt
¼ cup Plain Chia Pudding (page 33)
3–4 vegan breakfast sausages (I like MorningStar Farms, or use what you like)
Generous drizzle of agave
½ cup or more of your kid's favorite berries (Yaqeen likes strawberries)
Box Banana Bread, a couple of slices (page 217)
Maple syrup for the sausage

1. In a small bowl, mix the yogurt and chia pudding; set aside. Cook your sausage according to the package directions. Put a serving of chia pudding in a compartment of your kiddo's lunch box with a drizzle of agave. Add the berries and banana bread. Once the sausage is cooked, add it to the lunch box as well, with a little bit of maple syrup for dipping, and wish your kid a good day and a happy belly from me!

All-American Kiddo Lunch

MAKES 1 SERVING

This is such a familiar pairing. It's mild and tasty—perfect for a growing palate. I make this lunch with our leftover mac and cheese and chicken nuggets (always a winner) and toss in some garlic green beans to brighten the whole thing up. Serve with a small glass of oat milk, and you'll have a very happy kid.

1 serving Simply Good Southern Mac and Cheese (page 106)
4–6 vegan chicken nuggets (I like Impossible Wild Nuggies)
1–2 teaspoons plant butter (I like Country Crock)
½ cup or more fresh or frozen green beans
1 tablespoon water
Pinch of chopped fresh garlic
Salt and pepper
1–2 ounces ketchup, for dipping
Oat milk, for drinking

1. Heat up the mac and cheese and cook the chicken nuggets according to the package directions.
2. Heat a nonstick pan to medium heat and put in the butter and green beans. Toss the beans in the pan to coat with butter. Add the water and cook for 2–3 minutes, or until the water evaporates. Add the garlic and cook for another minute or so; turn off the heat.
3. Plate the mac and cheese, nuggets, and beans (or pack them into your kiddo's lunch box). Serve with ketchup and a glass of cold oat milk.

Tame the Hunger Monster Grilled Cheese and Easy Tomato Soup

MAKES 4 SERVINGS

I borrowed this tasty little lunch from one of my neighbors. This is a quintessential comforting favorite for all ages, not just kiddos. Say yes, please, to healthy calories, protein, carbs, and fiber with this easy vegan version of a classic: this recipe even has a throwback of Campbell's added in for a little sweetness. This will definitely knock the hunger monster out!

1 can tomato soup (Campbell's or your favorite brand)
1 quart prepared tomato soup (I like Pacific)
Cooking spray
8 slices vegan sharp Cheddar cheese
8 slices bread (your favorite sandwich bread)
Fruit and oat milk, for serving

1. In a soup pot, place both the can and quart of tomato soup; allow to slowly warm over medium heat.
2. Heat a pan to medium heat, spray with cooking spray, and place 1 slice of cheese covered with 1 slice of bread in the pan, cheese-side down; the cooking oil will prevent the cheese from sticking. Melt the cheese for about 1 minute, and then carefully flip the sandwich over so the bread side is down. Allow the bread side to toast for 2–3 minutes or until golden-brown. Add the other piece of bread on top, and flip the sandwich over to toast the other side (you may need to spray more cooking oil). Allow the second side to cook until the bread is golden-brown and the cheese is all melty. Repeat with each sandwich.
3. Make your kiddo's lunch complete by adding some dried mango, fresh blueberries, and a glass of oat milk on the side.

COOK'S NOTE: Vegan cheese does not melt like traditional cheese; it requires an additional step.

mushie

Papa's Black Beans and Veggie Rice with Sweet Plantains (Maduros)

MAKES 4 SERVINGS

Black beans and rice along with plantains and avocado, with cantaloupe and trail mix for a snack, is one of my nephew's absolute favorite meals—and it should be, since it includes all his favorite foods. This meal will make both you and your little ones happy: the yummy stewed black beans are packed with calories and protein and pair well with the veggies snuggled in with the rice. The sweet plantains are loaded with fiber and vitamins A, C, and B-6. Add sliced avocado, cantaloupe, and trail mix for a nice fat and fiber boost for a little body.

3 tablespoons avocado oil
½ cup minced onion
1 teaspoon minced garlic
1 cup chopped soft, super-ripe tomato
1 teaspoon adobo seasoning
1 teaspoon sea salt
2 (15.5-ounce) cans black beans plus their liquid
1 cup long-grain white rice
2 cups water
¼ teaspoon sea salt
½ cup frozen mixed corn, peas, and carrots
1 large ripe plantain
½ cup cooking oil (avocado, safflower, or canola)
1 tablespoon chopped fresh cilantro, for garnish (optional)
Avocado slices, cubed cantaloupe, and trail mix, for serving

1. Heat the avocado oil in a medium to large pan (not a pot) to medium high. Add the onion and garlic, and sauté until they start to turn golden-brown, for 2–3 minutes. Add the tomato, adobo seasoning, and salt, and let the tomato stew down until it gets super mushy, for 6–8 minutes or more. Add the beans and their liquid and cook for about 15 minutes until the tomato cooks and the beans soften.
With a wooden spoon, smash some of the beans to thicken juices and add flavor. You should have a thick black bean stew when done.
2. To make the rice, combine the rice, water, salt, and the mixed veggies in a small saucepan. Cover and cook the rice according to package directions.
3. While the rice cooks, prepare the plantains. Line a plate with paper towels and set aside. Peel and slice the plantain at an angle, about 1 inch thick. Heat a sauté pan with the oil over medium-high heat. Add the plantains and fry until golden-brown, for 2–3 minutes, flipping to ensure both sides are cooked. Transfer to the paper towel–lined plate to drain excess oil.
4. Make your kiddo's lunch box with a generous portion of black beans and a scoop of rice plus 3–4 plantain pieces. Garnish with the cilantro, if desired. Add the avocado, some cantaloupe, and your favorite energy-boosting trail mix for a snack.

Auntie's Tofu Chili Cornbread

MAKES 4 SERVINGS

This lunch sounds like a warm fall hug to me and is super comforting for your kiddo as they work to get back into the swing of the school year. Chili can be a yummy superfood, packed with tons of protein, nutrients, and fiber. This makes a family-size pot of chili. We have chili a few nights a week, and I like to use the leftovers for school lunch or for lunch at home anytime. It freezes well too. Serve this with apple slices and a Chocolate Chunk Fudgie Brownie (page 203) for a really big hug!

¼ cup avocado oil or your favorite cooking oil (avocado, safflower, or canola)
½ pound of extra-firm tofu, crumbled
½ cup chopped onion
½ tablespoon minced garlic
2 tablespoons chili powder
1½ teaspoons sea salt
½ teaspoon pepper
1½ teaspoons ground cumin
1½ teaspoons dried oregano
½ cup diced green bell pepper
1 (15-ounce) can whole tomatoes
1 cup vegan chicken stock
½ cup water
¼ cup tomato sauce
1 (28-ounce) can chili beans, rinsed and drained
1 tablespoon chopped fresh cilantro (optional)
Avocado slices, Jalapeño Dip (page 12), and cornbread, for serving

1. In a soup or stockpot on medium high, add the avocado oil. Cook the crumbled tofu for 12–15 minutes until all the water is cooked off and the tofu starts to turn golden-brown. Add the onion and garlic and cook for another 3–4 minutes, or until the onions soften and become translucent. Season with chili powder, salt, pepper, cumin, and oregano. Add the bell pepper and whole tomatoes, breaking a few tomatoes into pieces, and then add the stock, water, and tomato sauce. Finally, add the beans and cook for 30 minutes, or until the beans split and the chili thickens. About 5 minutes before the chili is done, add the cilantro, if desired. Serve with the avocado, Jalapeño Dip, and cornbread—or whatever you like!

Hidden Veggie Pasta with Nut-Butter Cracker Sandwiches

MAKES 4 SERVINGS

My nephew has decided he does not eat anything green, so I have learned to outsmart him. While I understand this recipe does not contain a ton of veggies, it's a good start to coaxing your kiddo to eat some vegetables. Hey, the struggle is real trying to get veggies into those little bodies, so I will take what I can get! The veggies add fiber and other nutrients; they also add a nice sweetness and mellowness to the sauce, perfect for picky little palates. Pack with old-school nut-butter sandwiches and some sweet antioxidant-rich strawberry slices.

1 cup frozen veggies (I like a blend of peas, carrots, and corn)
1 (15-ounce) can tomato sauce
2 cups water
¾ cup vegan Cheddar cheese shreds, or about 5 slices (I like Violife)
¼ teaspoon sea salt plus a couple of pinches
2 tablespoons avocado oil
¼ teaspoon Italian seasoning
2 pinches granulated onion
1 teaspoon agave (optional; the veggies will add a natural sweetness)
1½ cups rigatoni

1. Heat a medium saucepot on medium heat and put in the frozen veggies, tomato sauce, water, cheese, salt, oil, Italian seasoning, granulated onion, and agave, if using. Bring to a simmer and cook for about 5 minutes until the veggies are tender. Then remove from the heat. Add everything to a blender and blend until smooth. Return the blend to the pot and add the dry uncooked pasta. Simmer on low for about 35 minutes, or until the pasta is done. You will end up with a thick, creamy, yummy all-over-the-pasta sauce.

Nut-Butter Cracker Sammies

MAKES 5 SANDWICHES

Sunflower butter is made from little nutrient-dense sunflower seeds, which are a great source of protein, healthy fats, vitamin E, and magnesium. The protein and healthy fats will keep your little one satiated and feeling full and energized for playtime.

10 of your kid's favorite crackers
¼ cup or more sunflower butter (peanut butter is fine too, if your kiddo can eat it)
Strawberries, sliced, for serving

1. Spread each cracker with a teaspoon or two of sunflower or peanut butter and top with the second cracker for your little one's lunch box or snack time.
2. To assemble your kiddo's lunch, scoop a generous portion of pasta into a section of the lunch box that keeps the food warm. Place the nut-butter cracker sandwiches in another section and the strawberries in a final compartment.

Blackened Tofu Burgers with Sliced Avocado and Strawberries

MAKES 2 SERVINGS

The alternate name for these burgers is Flavor Bombs. But they also have plenty of protein for growing (and grown!) bodies: the tofu alone has a whopping 10 grams of protein per 3-ounce serving. Pan-fry the tofu and throw it on your kid's favorite bun with a smear of ketchup and you won't hear a peep until they are done. Avocado slices and strawberries—full of vitamin C, potassium, antioxidants, and carbohydrates—are a perfect rich and sweet accompaniment.

2–4 pieces Pan-Fried Cajun Butter Blackened Tofu (page 105)
2 burger buns
Ketchup
1 avocado, sliced
A handful of strawberries

1. Cook the tofu according to the Pan-Fried Cajun Butter Blackened Tofu recipe.
2. Build burgers on a soft bun of your choice, and dress as your kiddo likes. Pack the lunch box with as many avocado slices and strawberries as your kiddo will eat.

Black Pepper Chicken Fried Tofu with Cheesy Steamed Broccoli and Carrots

MAKES 3–4 SERVINGS

A 3-ounce serving of the tofu has a whopping 10 grams of protein while the broccoli and carrot have just about every vitamin and mineral in the alphabet. I like to cut the tofu into nugget-size pieces and add some ketchup to the plate too. As for the veggies? If you put enough cheese sauce on them, your kiddo may not even complain about the green stuff on the plate. Add some sliced oranges and apples, and you've fueled that little body well.

FOR THE CHEESY SAUCE

1 cup mature or regular vegan Cheddar cheese (I like Violife)
1½ cups vegan provolone (I like Violife)
1½ cups plain, unsweetened plant milk (I like soy)
¼ teaspoon salt
1 tablespoon minced pimiento pepper (optional but recommended)

FOR THE BLACK PEPPER CHICKEN FRIED TOFU

1 pound extra-firm tofu (I like House Foods)
½–1 teaspoon adobo seasoning
¼ teaspoon chili powder
¼ teaspoon onion powder
1 cup Mild Black Pepper Breading (page 16)
1 cup plain, unsweetened plant milk (I like soy, or use your favorite plant milk)
1 cup cooking oil (avocado, safflower, or canola)
1 small package frozen broccoli
1 small package frozen carrots
Apple and orange slices, for serving

1. In a small saucepan, heat the Cheddar, provolone, and milk over medium. Allow the cheese and milk to combine and melt, for 7–10 minutes. Once well combined into a nice thick sauce, add the salt. Whisk the sauce until all the lumps and bumps are gone. Then add the pimiento peppers. It's ready to use now, or it can be stored in the fridge for 5–7 days.

COOK'S NOTE: When the sauce is chilled, it may take on the consistency of jelly; simply warm it back up to get a smoother sauce.

2. Tear or cut the tofu into bite-size pieces about 1 inch or so in size. In a small mixing bowl, combine the tofu and season with adobo, chili powder, and onion powder; set aside. In another bowl, place the milk, and in a third bowl, place the black pepper breading.
3. Working in batches, dredge the seasoned tofu first through the breading, then in the milk, and then back to the breading. Shake any excess breading from the tofu pieces.
4. Heat a sauté pan with the cooking oil. Carefully lower the breaded tofu pieces into the hot oil. Fry until golden-brown on each side, for 2–3 minutes. You can also fry in an air fryer; follow the manufacturer's instructions.
5. While the tofu is frying, empty the broccoli and carrots into a saucepan and cook as directed on the package.
6. To assemble your kiddo's lunch, pile a plate high with tofu with a good amount of carrots and broccoli and an even bigger amount of warm cheese sauce. Serve apple and orange slices on the side.

"Reel Fun Movie Playdate" a.k.a. Mac and Cheese, Corn Dogs, and Dippers

MAKES 4 SERVINGS

A kids' movie night is a terrific way for children to bond, have fun, and get lost in the magic of storytelling on the big screen. What's better than hanging with friends and making memories? The corn dogs and mac and cheese are sure to please. Throw in some microwave or stovetop popcorn, and you will have a happy crowd.

Simply Good Southern Mac and Cheese (page 106)
4 MorningStar Veggie Corn Dogs
1 cup carrots and celery, sliced
Vegan Ranch (page 18)
1 or 2 oranges, cut into wedges

1. Cook the mac and cheese according to the recipe. Cook the corn dogs according to the package directions.
2. To prepare for movie night, divide the mac and cheese into four portions, add the corn dogs, and serve with the carrots and celery with Vegan Ranch and some orange wedges. I like to add a bowl of popcorn for movie night!

JUST Fried Egg and Cheese Sandwiches

MAKES 2 SANDWICHES

This is admittedly a little kid's lunch: it's super mild, and you can have a lot of fun making little sandwich fingers. I made these when my nephew was in pre-K. I would give him a cookie, some oat milk, and orange slices. And then just pray he would eat the avocado and tomato!

- 4 JUST Egg folds, or ¼ cup JUST Egg liquid, cooked to omelet squares
- Cooking spray
- 4 slices bread (your favorite sandwich bread)
- 4 slices vegan sharp Cheddar cheese
- ¼ cup cherry tomatoes
- ½ avocado, sliced
- 1 orange, sliced
- 1 Auntie's Salted Chocolate Chip Cookies (page 205), or whatever cookie your little one likes

1. Cook the JUST Egg folds according to the package directions.
2. Heat a nonstick pan and spray with cooking oil. To make one sandwich, place one slice of bread in the pan. Add one slice of Cheddar on top, followed by the egg, and then a second slice of cheese. Add the top slice of bread, then cover and toast on medium-low heat, checking frequently. Flip and toast the other side. It should take 5–7 minutes for the cheese to fully melt.
3. Serve your little one the egg sammies with as many cherry tomatoes and slices of avocado and oranges as they will eat. Plus one cookie!

Chick'n Noodle Soup Leftovers with Cornbread

MAKES 1 SERVING

I am in love with those expensive kiddie bento boxes for just this kind of a lunch. You can send your little one off with comforting chick'n noodle soup loaded with protein, minerals, fiber, and clean and healthy fats. Round it out with a side of cornbread, bananas, and mango. This lunch is like a warm hug!

1 serving Slow Cooker Chick'n Noodle Soup (page 115)
1 cornbread muffin (Box Cornbread/Muffins, page 30)
1 banana, cut into about 4 pieces with the skin on
½ cup fresh mango, cubed

1. When ready to make your kiddo's lunch, pour some really hot water into a soup canteen and set it aside to warm. While it is warming, heat the soup. Dump the water from the canteen and pour in the soup. In the remaining compartments of your kiddo's lunch box, place the cornbread muffin, banana, and mango.

Pan-Fried Adobo Tofu

MAKES 2–3 SERVINGS

"Auntie, can you make me some tofu and ketchup?" I promise you, I hear that multiple times a week! And I love hearing it. Tofu is loaded with goodness; it has a whopping 10 grams of protein per 3-ounce serving. Serve with any veggie side, along with cantaloupe, and you have another delicious, nutritious meal.

½ teaspoon granulated onion
½ teaspoon chili powder
½ teaspoon adobo seasoning
¼ teaspoon sea salt
1 pound extra-firm tofu
¼ cup avocado oil

1. In a small spice bowl, place the granulated onion, chili powder, adobo seasoning, and salt; mix and set aside.
2. Cut your tofu into about 16 squares, roughly 1½ by 1½ inches. Lay the tofu out on a plate or tray and season one side with the seasoning mixture; flip and season the other side. Allow to set for a few minutes. In a pinch, you can use just the adobo seasoning, and it will be fine.
3. When ready to cook, heat a medium pan to medium high; put in the cooking oil and cook the tofu squares in batches. Make sure the squares sizzle when they hit the pan. You can cover the pan and cook for 2–3 minutes per side until the tofu is nice and crispy. Remove from the pan and set aside until ready to serve with a veggie side.

Mama-Made Pepperoni Pizza Pockets with Buttery Sweet Peas

MAKES 4–6 POCKETS

I have to admit I was thinking of those frozen pizza pockets we all know and love when I made these. Why not try a healthier version of a childhood favorite? I really like the flavor of Field Roast's pepperoni; I think it gets really close to the original version. The side dish of peas is a good source of vitamins and antioxidants, which will keep your little one's immune system strong. Serve the pockets with blueberries and bananas, and you're giving your kiddo fiber and more vitamins and minerals, including potassium and magnesium, both of which act as electrolytes. Bonus: this is easy and quick to make—and it makes for happy campers.

Cooking spray
1 sheet puff pastry
1¼ cups marinara sauce (jarred or recipe on page 19)
1½ cups shredded vegan mozzarella
1 tablespoon chopped fresh parsley or basil (optional)
1 tablespoon warm water
1 teaspoon egg (I like Ener-G Egg Replacer)
1–2 packages plant-based pepperoni (I like Field Roast Plant-Based Pepperoni Slices)
Sweet peas, blueberries, and banana slices, for serving

1. Preheat the oven to 400°F. Spray a cookie sheet or baking pan with cooking spray.
2. Roll out your puff pastry to a 10 x 12-inch rectangle, then cut it into six 4 x 6-inch smaller rectangles and set aside on the baking pan. In a small mixing bowl, combine the marinara, cheese, and parsley, if using, and mix.
3. In a small bowl, mix the warm water and egg to make your egg wash; set aside.
4. Lay 3–5 pieces of pepperoni on the bottom half of each rectangle of puff pastry, leaving about ⅜ inch on the bottom and sides, and then add about ¼ cup of the cheese mixture. Using a small paintbrush or your finger, paint all four ⅜-inch sides with the egg wash to seal. Fold over the top half of the pastry rectangle and press closed, using a fork to completely seal all three sides or the cheese will cook out. Lay all six pockets on the oiled baking pan and cook for 15 minutes. While the pockets are cooking, make the peas (see page 184).
5. To make your kiddo's lunch, give them one or two hot pockets, a generous amount of sweet peas, a handful of blueberries, and the banana.

Buttery Sweet Peas

MAKES 2–3 SERVINGS

Sweet peas are such a nostalgic veggie. I love them because they are mild and add a much-needed boost of fiber to little bellies. They have a number of vitamins, among them B, C, and K, and a good amount of iron and magnesium as well. You can't go wrong with this lovely little veggie.

2 tablespoons butter (I prefer Country Crock Plant Butter)
1 teaspoon fresh garlic
2 cups frozen green peas
½ cup frozen edamame (optional)
½ teaspoon natural cane sugar
¼ teaspoon sea salt
6 tablespoons water

1. Put a medium sauté pan on medium-high heat. Put in the butter, garlic, and peas, plus edamame, if using. Toss until the butter is melted and the peas and edamame are bright green, for 2–3 minutes. Season with sugar and salt and add the water. Allow to steam-cook for a total of about 5 minutes.

Lunch Box Ginger Ramen with Scrambled Egg and Steamed Edamame

MAKES 2–3 SERVINGS

Kids love noodles (I think it's the squiggliness of them)! If you have a little foodie on your hands, they may appreciate this lightly Asian-inspired lunch, curated just for them. The ramen is fun to eat and flavorful; the edamame is packed with protein, potassium, fiber, and iron. Add a little natural fat from some avocado and JUST Egg and serve with sliced oranges full of vitamin C, and your kiddo has a pretty complete meal.

2 packs Instant Ramen noodles
2 teaspoons sesame oil
Heaping ½ teaspoon minced garlic
1 teaspoon peeled and grated or minced fresh ginger
2 tablespoons light soy sauce
½ teaspoon sriracha
1¼ teaspoons light-brown sugar
¼ teaspoon toasted sesame seeds
1 cup reserved pasta water
1¼ tablespoons sliced green onion, plus more for garnish
2 tablespoons avocado oil
2 cups edamame beans shelled or in pods, thawed
½ teaspoon sea salt
½ teaspoon chopped fresh garlic (optional)
1 tablespoon tamari or soy sauce (optional)
3–4 tablespoons JUST Egg
Avocado, cubed, for serving
Oranges, sliced, for serving

1. In a medium soup pot over medium-high heat, cook the ramen for 1 minute, just until it's soft and pliable. Remove the noodles from the water and set aside. Reserve 1 cup of the pasta water.
2. In a medium pan, heat the sesame oil over medium heat. Add the garlic and ginger and allow to brown very lightly, just for a minute or so. Add the soy sauce, sriracha, sugar, and sesame seeds, and then add the ramen and pasta water to the pan. Toss to coat and garnish with green onions.
3. Heat a medium pan with the avocado oil over medium-high heat. Then add the edamame, salt, and chopped garlic, if using; toss, allowing 1–2 minutes for the edamame to cook. Lightly season with salt, then add the tamari, if using. Turn off heat.
4. Cook the JUST Egg according to the package directions (see Pan-Fried Eggs on page 63).
5. To keep the lunch warm, put the noodles on the bottom of an insulated hot-food container and top with a layer of edamame and fried egg. I like to include some cubed avocado and orange slices on the side.

Chicken Burgers with Green Bean Fries

MAKES 4 BURGERS

My nephew really enjoys Next Level Burger's chicken burger, so I decided to try to make one myself. I love serving these with green bean fries for more nutrition, along with avocado and watermelon slices and trail mix for additional healthy fats, fiber, and minerals—great for muscle building and heart health.

4 vegan chicken patties (I like MorningStar Farms Original Chik'n Patties)
4 burger buns
Ketchup (or other sauces or dressings)
1 avocado, sliced
Lettuce, tomato, cucumber, or whatever veggie your little one will eat
Cubed watermelon and trail mix, for serving

1. Cook the chicken patties according to the package directions. Allow them to cool a bit and place them on the buns with ketchup. Add the avocado and any veggie you can get away with! Pack your kiddo's lunch box with the burger, green bean fries (see recipe below), watermelon, and a little packet of trail mix.

Green Bean Fries

I didn't want to serve these burgers with just any old fries, so I went green: green beans are high in vitamin K, and they also contain a decent amount of calcium. These nutrients are important for maintaining strong, healthy bones and reducing risk of fractures in little bodies.

1 pound package French green beans or regular green beans, trimmed
1 cup plain, unsweetened plant milk (I like soy)
½ teaspoon cider vinegar
2 cups Black Pepper Breading (page 16)
2 cups panko breadcrumbs
½ teaspoon sea salt
2 cups oil

1. Line a plate with paper towels and set aside.
2. Wash your green beans. Pat the remaining water off them and set aside to dry.
3. You will need three bowls. In one bowl, place the milk and vinegar and let set until the mixture thickens, for 1–2 minutes. Place the Black Pepper Breading in a second bowl and set aside. In a third bowl, combine the panko and salt and mix well. Working in small batches, dredge the green beans: first in the milk, then in the breading, then back in the milk, and then in the panko.
4. Heat the oil in a deep pot. Then drop the coated beans into the hot oil and cook until they start to float and turn a rich golden-brown. Remove them from the oil and place on the paper towel–lined plate. Pack these beans in your kiddo's lunch or serve with your favorite dipping sauce.

COOK'S NOTE: You can air-fry, oven-fry, or pan-fry these. To air-fry, follow manufacturer's instructions. To pan-fry on the stovetop, heat cooking oil in a frying pan or small pot on medium heat. When the oil is ready, it will appear thinner and start to shimmer; cook the beans for 5–10 minutes.

Shredded or Broken Tofu Tacos

MAKES 4 SERVINGS

I made these tacos as part of a fifth-grade field trip to my restaurant for the kids at my nephew's school. Well, I didn't make them all by myself. Thirty-three fifth graders descended on my kitchen, bringing all their bubbly, curious, sweet, exuberant, and fun energy to this brand-new (for some) experience of cooking vegan food. I gave them this recipe, and we dove in. Once all the dust had settled, they had made these delicious tacos to eat. For dessert, the kids had Strawberry Shortcake (page 213). This is a great lunch for your big kid or a meal for the whole family. The taco filling is a great make-ahead mixture to have in your fridge for a quick dinner.

2 pounds tofu
2 cups plus 1 tablespoon cooking oil (avocado, safflower, or canola)
1 cup minced onion
1 cup minced red bell pepper
2 teaspoons chopped fresh garlic
2 cups veggie stock
1 (15-ounce) can crushed tomatoes
1 tablespoon chili powder
2½ teaspoons cumin
2½ teaspoons sea salt
1 teaspoon natural cane sugar
¾ teaspoon garlic powder
½ teaspoon onion powder
¼ teaspoon freshly ground black pepper
1 package corn tortillas or taco shells
1 small head iceberg lettuce, shredded
1 cup or more diced tomatoes
½ cup or more Jalapeño Dip (page 12)
Diced avocado and fresh fruit, for serving

1. Using a grater, grate your tofu or use your hands to break the tofu into pieces that resemble crumbled feta cheese. Heat the 2 cups of cooking oil in a medium pan or pot on medium-high heat. Then, working in batches, cook the tofu crumbles until they are golden-brown and start to float. If you are using crumbled tofu, cook for 12–15 minutes. If your tofu is shredded, cook for about half that time. Once the tofu is done, it will be crisp and should sound like cereal going into a bowl. (You can also skip the stovetop and air-fry your tofu.) Remove the tofu and place on a paper towel–lined tray.
2. Once all the tofu is fried, reserve ¼ cup of hot oil and add it to a sauté pan. Heat the pan over medium-high heat and add the onion, red bell pepper, and garlic; sauté until the onions start to turn translucent. Pour in the stock and crushed tomatoes, and season with chili powder, cumin, salt, sugar, garlic powder, onion powder, and black pepper. Add the extra tablespoon of oil. Cook for 20–25 minutes, or until the mixture is slightly dry.
3. To make the tacos, heat the tortillas and fill with the tofu mixture. Top with the lettuce and tomatoes, with a little Jalapeño Dip on the side. Serve with the avocado and fruit.

Bacon Chicken Pasta Bake Leftovers with Garlic Bread

MAKES 1 SERVING

This is a great lunch box leftover! Just make the Chicken Pasta Bake (page 113) for supper, and make sure you have leftovers for lunch the next day. There is nothing like a yummy pasta to replenish some of the energy spent chasing everything that moves throughout the day, as many little children do (goddess, their pace is dizzying)! This is a carb-heavy lunch; however, carbs from a variety of whole-grain pastas and breads can be a main source of energy for a little body. These carbs help fuel the brain, kidneys, heart muscles, and central nervous system. Serve with orange slices and baby carrots, and you will give your kiddo vitamins plus fiber and beta-carotene for another healthy meal.

Chicken Pasta Bake (page 113)
Garlic bread (page 33)
Orange slices
Baby carrots

1. Prepare the Chicken Pasta Bake and garlic bread according to the recipes. To make your kiddo's lunch, give them a serving of pasta along with garlic bread and as many orange slices and carrots as they will eat.

Baba's Smoked Tofu Cold Cuts Sammie

MAKES 4 SANDWICHES

Cold sandwiches are a great option for kiddos' school lunches—or let's face it, adult lunches too. These sandwiches are simple and quick and bursting with flavor.

Papa's Sammie Sauce (page 13)
8 slices sandwich bread
Iceberg lettuce
1 extra-large heirloom or regular tomato, sliced
½ pound tofu, sliced thin like cold cuts (I like Baba's Mesquite Smoked Tofu, or use your favorite flavored tofu)

1. Spread the sammie sauce on one slice of bread. Add a piece or two of a soft, crisp lettuce like iceberg, then add the tomatoes and top with 2–3 pieces of tofu. Top with another slice of bread and enjoy!

Auntie's Meaty Kid-Pleasin' Lasagna

MAKES 1 FAMILY-SIZE PAN OF LASAGNA

When I was growing up, we made—and ate!—a lot of lasagna. We always used tofu and veggies. This recipe is full of veggies, but it uses plant meat rather than tofu. I like Impossible, but use your favorite. This lasagna will make plenty for a few days; to change it up, serve with a Simple Bag Salad (page 113) one night and add some garlic bread (page 33) the next. However you serve it, you'll have a delicious meal for the entire family.

FOR THE RAGÙ SAUCE

6 tablespoons olive oil
1½ cups minced yellow onion
1½ tablespoons minced garlic
1½ pounds ground plant meat (I like Impossible)
3 teaspoons Italian seasoning
3 teaspoons sea salt
¾ teaspoon freshly ground black pepper
3 cups cherry tomatoes, halved
3 (15-ounce) cans tomato sauce
2½ teaspoons natural cane sugar
¾ cup vegan cream cheese (I like Violife)

FOR THE FILLING

2 tablespoons extra-virgin olive oil
2 pints mushrooms, sliced
1 teaspoon minced garlic
Salt and pepper
½ bag or more fresh spinach leaves, 2–3 cups
1 package lasagna
Plant butter for coating
¼ cup grated vegan Parmesan cheese, plus more for garnish
5 or more cups shredded vegan mozzarella (I like Violife)
1 teaspoon minced fresh flat-leaf parsley, for garnish

MAKE THE RAGÙ

1. Heat a large pot over medium-high heat. Put the olive oil in the pot and swirl to evenly coat. Add the onion, garlic, and plant meat, then stir in the Italian seasoning, salt, and pepper. Cook the mixture, stirring frequently, until softened and starting to caramelize, for about 3 minutes. Add the cherry tomatoes and cook until the tomatoes soften and start to burst, for another 2–3 minutes. Pour in the tomato sauce, reduce the heat to medium, add the sugar and cream cheese, and cook, stirring, until slightly reduced, for 6–8 minutes.

MAKE THE FILLING

1. In a sauté pan, heat the olive oil on medium-high heat. Add the mushrooms, garlic, and a generous pinch of salt and pepper, and sauté for about 2 minutes or until fragrant. Add the spinach and allow to wilt—no more than a minute so it retains some firmness.

COOK THE PASTA

1. Bring a large pot of water with some salt to a boil. Add the lasagna noodles and let them cook, checking frequently so that you can take them off the heat once they're done, in about 10 minutes. You want to make sure that the outer layer of the noodles is soft while the inner core is just a little bit stiff.

MAKE THE LASAGNA

1. Preheat the oven to 350°F.
2. Coat a 9 x 13-inch baking dish with plant butter. Spread ¾ cup of the ragù in the prepared baking dish. Top with a layer of noodles followed by the mushroom filling, and then a layer of cheeses. Repeat for 2–3 more layers, starting with the noodles and ending with the ragù, mozzarella, and Parmesan on top.
3. Place the baking dish on a rimmed baking sheet, and bake the lasagna until bubbling and beginning to brown on top, 50–60 minutes. Let the lasagna sit for 45 minutes before serving. Garnish with parsley.

Quesadillas and Tajín Butter Street Corn

MAKES 6 SERVINGS

This recipe is super fun to make with your kids during grilling season since corn is one of the first foods a lot of kids love. And who does not like a quesadilla!? In addition to the flavorful kick of the corn, this recipe uses two proteins—tofu and plant beef—for an enjoyable flavor and texture combination. The freshness of the tofu and the richness of the plant meat gives you the best of many vegan worlds here—not to mention the cheese.

- **4–6 ears of corn, shucked**
- **1 pound firm tofu**
- **6 tablespoons cooking oil (avocado, safflower, or canola), divided**
- **¼ cup minced onion**
- **2 teaspoons chopped fresh garlic**
- **½ pound ground plant meat (I like Impossible)**
- **2 teaspoons chili powder**
- **2 teaspoons ground cumin**
- **2 teaspoons dried oregano**
- **¼ cup soy sauce**
- **2 teaspoons sea salt**
- **¼ teaspoon red pepper flakes (optional)**
- **2 tablespoons chopped fresh cilantro**
- **1 (16-ounce) package prewashed and cut fajita veggie mix, or two bell peppers (green and red) and 1 red onion, julienned**
- **6 flour tortillas**
- **1–2 tablespoons melted plant butter**
- **2 cups shredded vegan Cheddar and mozzarella cheese (I like Daiya Cheddar & Mozza Shreds, or use your favorite brand)**
- **½ cup or more Tajín Butter (page 14)**
- **Lime wedges, for serving**

1. Preheat a grill or grill pan to medium high. Grill the corn, turning often, until slightly charred all over, for about 8 minutes. Keep the corn in a warm oven until the quesadillas are done.
2. Using your hands, squeeze all the water out of the tofu and set aside.
3. Heat a medium skillet or pan with a thin coating of cooking oil over medium-high heat. Add the onion and garlic and cook until the garlic starts to brown and the onion turns slightly translucent. Crumble the tofu and plant meat into the pan and season with chili powder, cumin, dried oregano, soy sauce, salt, red pepper flakes, and cilantro. Cook for 4–6 minutes. Using a slotted spoon, remove the mixture from the pan and set it aside in a small bowl.
4. Heat the remaining oil in the same skillet. Add the fajita veggie mix and sauté until tender, for about 5 minutes. Add to the bowl with the tofu mixture and toss.
5. Wipe the skillet clean with a paper towel and reduce the heat to medium. Brush one side of the tortillas with the butter. To assemble the quesadillas, put one tortilla, buttered-side down, in the skillet. Sprinkle ⅓ cup cheese on top of the tortilla and top with about ⅓ cup of the tofu mixture. Fold the top half over and cook until golden-brown on the bottom; carefully flip the quesadilla and cook until the opposite side is golden-brown. Repeat with the rest of the tortillas.
6. Once the quesadillas are ready, remove the corn from the oven. Brush the corn with a layer of Tajín Butter. Serve warm with lime wedges.

The Sweetness of Life

I was on the road with Stevie, and he wanted cake. Well, to be honest, I was pulling my hair out, trying to make a cake, when his makeup artist came up to me and said, "Honey, go buy a box cake. Throw the box in the trash. Make the cake and bring it to him. You made it: it does not matter if it's a box or not!" He was right!

I mention that story here because it was a great lesson for me, and I hope a great lesson for you. A lot of people are too intimidated to make vegan baked goods. On top of that, I think a lot of people think of themselves as either savory cooks or bakers, but not both. Here's the good news: if you are a cook who thinks you can't bake, these recipes are for you (and yes, boxed mixes are OK!). If you are a baker who thinks, "I got this stuff down," these recipes are also for you (and yes, boxed mixes are OK!). I want this section to be all about empowering your dessert skills, no matter what they are. In this section, you'll find everything from a beautiful Bundt cake with cascading frosting to Strawberry Shortcake Ice-Cream Bars (get ready, seriously), and yummy pies, cookies, and brownies in between.

Chocolate Chunk Fudgie Brownies

MAKES 12 BROWNIES

If you have been vegan for a while, you know it is very hard to get a good—and I mean *good*—vegan fudge brownie. My trick here is to use big chocolate chunks to make fudgy bites throughout. I also add a small amount of espresso powder—not enough to caffeinate your kiddos but enough for a little special something to take these brownies over the top.

DRY INGREDIENTS

½ cup cocoa powder
1½ cups all-purpose flour
¾ cups dark-brown sugar
1 tablespoon espresso powder
1½ teaspoons sea salt
1 teaspoon baking powder
½ teaspoon baking soda

WET INGREDIENTS

1 cup plain, unsweetened milk (I like soy, or use your favorite plant milk)
½ cup applesauce
⅓ cup canola oil
2 tablespoons cider vinegar
1 teaspoon vanilla extract
½ cup dark chocolate, shaved
1 cup chopped dark chocolate, variably sized large pieces, for topping

1. Preheat the oven to 350°F. Spray or oil a 9 x 11-inch baking pan and set aside.

2. In a medium mixing bowl, place the cocoa powder, flour, brown sugar, espresso powder, salt, baking powder, and baking soda. Mix and set aside.

3. In a large mixing bowl, place the milk, applesauce, canola oil, vinegar, vanilla extract, and dark chocolate. Whisk all the ingredients together for a minute or so; add the dry ingredients to the wet and mix until well combined. Pour the mixture into the oiled pan. Sprinkle the chocolate chunks evenly across the top and give a slight swirl to distribute the chocolate evenly, leaving a good amount of chunks on top. Bake for 25–30 minutes.

Auntie's Salted Chocolate Chip Cookies

MAKES 12 COOKIES

My guy and I had salted chocolate chip cookies on vacation one year, and we fell in love with the mix of sweet and savory. It's hard to improve on simple perfection, but the addition of salt to a classic does just that. I hope you enjoy these as much as I do.

1¼ cups all-purpose flour
½ teaspoon baking soda
½ teaspoon baking powder
½ teaspoon sea salt
½ cup plant butter, room temperature
½ cup packed light-brown sugar
⅓ cup granulated sugar
2 teaspoons vanilla extract
3 tablespoons JUST Egg
1½ cups mini (or regular) chocolate chips
1 teaspoon or so flaky sea salt, for garnish

1. Preheat the oven to 350°F.

2. Sift the flour into a small bowl and add the baking soda, baking powder, and salt; stir to combine.

3. In a mixing bowl, place the butter, brown sugar, granulated sugar, vanilla extract, and JUST Egg. Whisk using an electric mixer or by hand until the sugar slightly dissolves and the texture of the mixture changes.

4. Add the dry ingredients to the wet and mix until combined, then fold in the chocolate chips. Scoop the dough into your desired size (I like a 1½-inch scoop) and place the scoops on a buttered cookie sheet. Bake for 10–12 minutes. Remove from the oven and sprinkle with salt.

My Sweet Georgia Peach

MAKES ONE 9-INCH PIE

The spring after my father died, my mother turned seventy-seven. We needed something to celebrate, so I rented a house on the coast, and the whole family came. I cooked all day; even my nephew helped a little bit. We had a feast, and my brother particularly loved this pie. My secret ingredient is the orange juice—and also love.

FOR THE OVERNIGHT PIECRUST

2½ cups all-purpose flour
1 teaspoon granulated sugar
1 teaspoon sea salt
½ cup plant butter, cold and broken into pieces
⅓ cup shortening (I like Spectrum Organic All Vegetable Shortening)
¼ cup ice-cold water

FOR THE FILLING

1 cup granulated sugar
1 cup orange juice
2 tablespoons freshly squeezed lemon juice, or juice of 1 lemon
½ teaspoon sea salt
1 teaspoon nutmeg
1 teaspoon cinnamon
1½ teaspoons vanilla extract
6 cups sliced ripe peaches, or about 8 average-size ripe peaches (if using canned peaches, drain the liquid; you can also use frozen peaches)
3 tablespoons cornstarch
2 tablespoons water
2 tablespoons plant butter

FOR THE MILK WASH

2 tablespoons oat milk
1 tablespoon agave
1 tablespoon coarse sugar for topping, if desired

Vanilla ice cream (I like Wicked Kitchen or Oatly! Vanilla Non-dairy Frozen Dessert), for serving

1. To make an overnight piecrust, place the flour, sugar, and salt in the bowl of an electric mixer with the whisk attachment. (If you don't have one, use a hand mixer or pastry cutter.) Add the butter and shortening and mix until the mixture turns into crumbly little balls. Add the water and mix again; the dough will start to pull together. Remove from the mixer and roll into a ball. Cover tightly in plastic and refrigerate overnight for the best results.

2. Preheat the oven to 350°F. Once the piecrust has set, remove it from the fridge and allow it to come to room temperature on the counter while you prepare the pie filling.

3. To make the filling, whisk together the sugar, orange juice, lemon juice, salt, nutmeg, cinnamon, and vanilla extract in a large saucepan. Add the peaches and bring to a boil on high heat. Reduce the heat to medium and cook until the peaches soften and split, for 18–20 minutes. Remove from the heat.

4. Make a slurry with the cornstarch and water, and add it to the peaches. Stir until the mixture starts to thicken. Add the butter and allow it to melt; stir the mixture until well combined. Set aside.

5. When the pie dough still feels a little hard in the center, break the ball in two and place one half in the fridge. Roll out the other half to about ⅛ inch thick to fit in a large deep-sided glass or ceramic pie dish with about a ½-inch overhang. If your filling is still cooking, place the pie dish with the bottom crust back in the fridge while you wait.

6. Once the pie filling is ready, spoon it into the prepared piecrust. You may or may not have some of the thickened juice left over, depending on how deep your pie dish is.

7. Grab the second half of the piecrust ball and roll it out about ½ inch wider in circumference than the width of your pie pan for a traditional flat pie top. Place this crust on top and crimp the edges to seal. For a fancier top-crust option, follow the lattice instructions below.

8. Mix the oat milk and agave and brush this wash over the flat pie top or lattice and sprinkle with coarse sugar, if desired.

9. Bake for 45–50 minutes, or until the top is golden-brown. Cool completely before serving. Serve à la mode with vanilla ice cream.

FANCY-ISH LATTICE INSTRUCTIONS

1. Once you've rolled the top piecrust out, cut it into ¾-inch-wide strips. Lay the first two strips in an X on top of the pie. Alternate horizontal and vertical strips, weaving them in an over-and-under pattern. Use your shortest strips for the edges of the lattice. Trim the edges and crimp the ends of the strips together with the bottom crust.

Vanilla Caramel Apple Sprinkle Ice-Cream Sammies

MAKES 12 SANDWICHES

An ice-cream sandwich is a treat almost no one can say no to. I first made these sammies on the road with Stevie, and he *loved* them. There were stops where I had time to make cookies, but there were definitely times when I had to buy a store-bought pack for the ice-cream sandwiches. I love the added benefit that Cybele's Free to Eat Confetti cookies are not only gluten-free, but they also leave out many known allergens. I have made this recipe for everyone from Stevie's band to kids for an ice-cream sprinkle party.

2 pints vegan vanilla ice cream
1 (1–2 ounce) package freeze-dried apples
½ cup or more vegan caramel sauce (I like Mr. Dewie's or Hey Boo)
4 boxes store-bought cookies (I like Cybele's Free to Eat Confetti Superb Cookies, or use your favorite brand)
Vegan sprinkles

1. Remove the ice cream from the freezer and allow it to soften, for no more than 10 minutes. Place the ice cream into a mixing bowl and stir until it has a thick batter-like consistency. Using a rolling pin, smash the freeze-dried apples into smaller pieces and fold into the ice-cream batter; drizzle with the caramel sauce. If your batter has become too soft, return to the freezer for 10–15 minutes, or until it is firm enough to scoop.

2. Lay your cookies out and scoop the ice cream onto a bottom cookie, about ¼ cup per cookie, and top with a second cookie. Place the cookies in the freezer as you make them so they're firmer before you roll on the sprinkles.

3. After about 20 minutes in the freezer, take the cookies out and roll the edge in your favorite color sprinkles. After rolling on the sprinkles, freeze the cookie sandwiches solid before serving for dessert or a sprinkle ice-cream cookie sandwich party.

Strawberry Shortcake with Skillet Jam and Whipped Cream

MAKES 6–12 SHORTCAKES

You know by now that I am a fan of making things easy. Well, nothing is easier than using a store-bought basic as a foundation for deliciousness. My secret ingredient here is Pillsbury Grands! Southern Homestyle Buttermilk Biscuits (yes, these are plant-based). Get a few containers of the biscuit mix, strawberries, and whipped cream, and you have all the makings for a delicious shortcake.

1–2 containers Pillsbury Grands! Southern Homestyle Buttermilk Biscuits
1 container plant-based whipped cream (I like Truwhip)
1 cup sliced fresh strawberries
Strawberry Skillet Jam (page 30)

1. Bake the biscuits according to the package directions; remove from the oven and allow to cool. When you're ready to make the shortcakes, start with a layer of strawberries followed by a layer of jam. Place your top biscuit, add another layer of jam, and top with whipped cream.

Granny's Apple Crisp à la Mode

MAKES 6 SERVINGS

I love anything apple pie and ice cream. This dessert saves you from rolling out a piecrust and still delivers all the flavor! In our house, we eat it hot out of the oven the first day, with a scoop of ice cream on top. Leftovers get mixed up with vanilla ice cream, and we have apple crisp à la mode ice-cream cups.

FOR THE FILLING

5 cups peeled, cored, and sliced Granny Smith apples (5–6 medium-size apples)
½ cup natural cane sugar
1 tablespoon cornstarch
2 teaspoons ground cinnamon
1 teaspoon nutmeg
Juice from 1 lemon
2 tablespoons plant butter

FOR THE TOPPING

½ cup quick-cooking oats
½ cup all-purpose flour
½ cup packed light-brown sugar
¼ teaspoon baking powder
¼ teaspoon baking soda
¼ cup melted plant butter
Vanilla ice cream (I prefer Oatly! or Wicked Kitchen for à la mode)

1. Preheat the oven to 350°F.
In a mixing bowl, place the apples, sugar, cornstarch, cinnamon, and nutmeg; toss the apples to coat well. Add the lemon juice and butter. Mix to break the butter up, and transfer the mixture to a 9-inch baking dish.
3. In another bowl, combine the oats, flour, brown sugar, baking powder, baking soda, and butter. Crumble evenly over the apple mixture. Bake at 350°F for about 45 minutes.
4. Remove from the oven and dish up. Serve with a scoop of ice cream and enjoy!

Box Banana Bread

MAKES 1 LOAF OR 12 MUFFINS

I love homemade breads as much as anyone, but let's face it, sometimes boxes are great too. You can make this from scratch, or you can grab a box from Trader Joe's: it's quick and easy and perfect for your breakfast or snack, your kiddo's lunch box, or anytime you want a not-too-sweet bite.

Cooking spray
1 banana
6 tablespoons JUST Egg
¾ cup oat milk or water
⅓ cup cooking oil (avocado, safflower, or canola)
1 box banana bread mix (I like Trader Joe's)

1. Preheat the oven to 350°F. Spray a loaf pan or pan of your choice with cooking spray. Set aside.

2. In a small mixing bowl, use a fork to mash the banana until relatively smooth. Add the egg and 2 tablespoons of the oat milk and mix until well combined. Add the oil and remaining milk; whisk well.

3. In a separate bowl, place the banana bread mixture and give it a stir to remove any lumps. Make a well and add the wet ingredients. Mix to combine (don't overmix).

4. Pour the mixture into the oiled pan and bake for 40 minutes if using a loaf pan (lessen time if using a flat pan), or until a toothpick inserted comes out dry.

Auntie's Secret Strawberry Box Bundt Cake with Lemon Cream Cheese Glaze

MAKES 1 CAKE

Don't be ashamed to buy a cake mix and make it your own. You are going to surprise yourself when you make this cake. It is so simple and comes out so beautifully. Just throw the box in the trash and let them eat cake!

Cooking spray
1 box Duncan Hines Perfectly Moist Strawberry Supreme cake mix
9 tablespoons JUST Egg
1 cup oat milk
½ cup canola oil

FOR THE LEMON CREAM CHEESE GLAZE AND TOPPING

4 ounces vegan cream cheese, room temperature (I like Violife)
½ cup powdered sugar, sifted
1 teaspoon vanilla extract
½ teaspoon lemon zest
¼ teaspoon lemon extract (optional)
3–4 tablespoons plant milk
¼ cup freeze-dried strawberries

1. Preheat the oven to 350°F. Spray a fancy Bundt pan with cooking spray and set aside.

2. Place the cake mix in a mixing bowl. In a separate bowl, place the egg, milk, and oil and whisk together. Add the egg mixture to the cake mix; mix until just combined, for a minute or so. Pour the mixture into the Bundt pan and bake for 30–35 minutes, or until a toothpick inserted comes out clean. If using another cake pan type or doubling the recipe, follow the package directions for baking times.

3. While the cake bakes, make the glaze. In a mixing bowl, place the cream cheese and beat or whisk until very smooth. Beat in the powdered sugar, then add the vanilla extract, lemon zest, and lemon extract, if using, and whisk until well combined. Pour in the milk and continue to whisk to the desired consistency. Put in the fridge and allow to set, for about 30 minutes.

4. While the glaze sets, put the freeze-dried strawberries in a resealable bag and, using a rolling pin or bottle of wine, smash the fruit into a fine powder or dust.

5. Remove the glaze from the fridge and allow it to soften up: it should be thick but pourable. Using a cake stand or whatever you have, pour the glaze over the cake as you turn it, doing your best to coat it evenly, and allow to set. Top with the strawberry dust and serve.

Fresh Blueberry Icebox Pie

MAKES ONE 9- OR 10-INCH PIE

This is for those days when you want pie, but turning on the oven is just too much. The flavor is really fresh, light, and bright. You can eat it on its own, but why would you when there is whipped cream? Add a little or a lot on top, and this icebox pie will make a satisfying and sweet ending to your day.

1 store-bought graham cracker crust
½ cup granulated sugar
2 tablespoons cornstarch
1 teaspoon vanilla extract
½ teaspoon cinnamon
½ teaspoon nutmeg
½ teaspoon dried ginger
Generous pinch of sea salt
Juice from 1 lemon
2 tablespoons water
1 tablespoon oat milk
4 cups fresh blueberries, divided
1 tablespoon plant butter
Plant-based whipped cream, for topping

1. Bake the store-bought piecrust according to the package directions and set aside.
2. In a large saucepan, place the sugar, cornstarch, vanilla extract, cinnamon, nutmeg, ginger, and salt and mix. Add the lemon juice, water, and oat milk and mix.
3. Heat the pan on medium heat and add 2½ cups of the blueberries to the mixture. Using the back of a sturdy spoon, smash about half the blueberries. Bring the mixture to a boil and continue cooking until thickened, for about 2 minutes. Add the butter and stir to combine. Set aside to cool.
4. Then fold in the remaining blueberries, and pour the mixture into the crust. Place the pie in the refrigerator to chill for 2 hours or until set.
5. Serve topped with whipped cream.

Strawberry Shortcake Ice-Cream Bars

MAKES 12 BARS

I don't like to be presumptuous, I really don't, but this dessert right here? Oh, you and everyone you know will fall in love with it! Most of the ingredients are from the corner store, and the memories are from childhood, with fresh fruit and ice cream all rolled into one delicious trip down memory lane for your taste buds.

COOK'S NOTE: I prepare this in a pan and cut it into small squares for serving.

- 3 pints vegan vanilla ice cream, divided (I like Wicked Kitchen or Oatly!)
- 1 (10-ounce) package vegan shortbread cookies (I like Lorna Doone)
- 2 (1.2-ounce) packages freeze-dried strawberries, divided
- 2 tablespoons light-brown sugar
- 6 tablespoons plant butter, melted
- 1½ cups Strawberry Skillet Jam (page 30) or your favorite strawberry jam
- 1 teaspoon vanilla extract or vanilla bean paste

1. Remove the ice cream from the freezer and allow to soften.

2. Line a square or rectangular baking pan with parchment paper, leaving a 2-inch overhang on all sides.

3. Put eight cookies in a resealable bag and, using a rolling pin or bottle of wine, crush them into coarse crumbs. Transfer to a medium bowl. Repeat with about a ½ cup or so of the freeze-dried strawberries. Add the ground berries to the crushed cookies. Mix and set aside.

4. Place the remaining freeze-dried strawberries in the resealable bag and roll until they become finely ground; transfer to another large bowl.

5. In the resealable bag, place the remaining cookies and the brown sugar and smash and roll until finely ground. Transfer to a third bowl. Add the butter and mix until the crumbs are coated. Press the mixture evenly into the bottom of the prepared pan.

6. Spoon the strawberry jam over the mixture in the pan and spread in an even layer. Cover the pan and put it in the freezer while you prepare the ice cream.

7. You will need two bowls: in one put 1 pint of the softened ice cream, and in the other put 2 pints of the ice cream. If you have an electric mixer, whisk both bowls of ice cream until they are thick and creamy and spreadable. (If you are using Wicked, it will become nicely fluffy.)
8. Add the freeze-dried strawberry powder and the vanilla extract to the bowl with the 2 pints of ice cream; mix well to incorporate and set back in the freezer.
9. Leave the bowl with the single pint of vanilla ice cream on your work surface.
10. Remove the pan from the freezer, and spread the pint of plain ice cream on top of the strawberry jam. Return to the freezer to set a bit. Once the ice cream is firm, in 20–25 minutes, bring it back to your work surface.
11. Remove the strawberry ice-cream mixture from the freezer and spread it on top of the plain vanilla ice-cream layer, making sure not to mix up the two layers of ice cream. Top with the crushed cookie-strawberry mixture from the first bowl you set aside. Cover and freeze until solid, for at least 6 hours and up to overnight.
12. Using the parchment overhang as handles, lift the ice-cream shortcake out of the pan and cut into squares.

Metric Conversions

The recipes in this book have not been tested with metric measurements, so some variations might occur.

Remember that the weight of dry ingredients varies according to the volume or density factor: 1 cup of flour weighs far less than 1 cup of sugar, and 1 tablespoon doesn't necessarily hold 3 teaspoons.

GENERAL FORMULAS FOR METRIC CONVERSIONS	
Ounces to grams	multiply ounces by 28.35
Grams to ounces	multiply ounces by 0.035
Pounds to grams	multiply pounds by 453.5
Pounds to kilograms	multiply pounds by 0.45
Cups to liters	multiply cups by 0.24
Fahrenheit to Celsius	subtract 32 from Fahrenheit temperature, multiply by 5, divide by 9
Celsius to Fahrenheit	multiply Celsius temperature by 9, divide by 5, add 32

VOLUME (LIQUID) MEASUREMENTS				
1 teaspoon	=	⅙ fluid ounce	=	5 milliliters
1 tablespoon	=	½ fluid ounce	=	15 milliliters
2 tablespoons	=	1 fluid ounce	=	30 milliliters
¼ cup	=	2 fluid ounces	=	60 milliliters
⅓ cup	=	2⅔ fluid ounces	=	79 milliliters
½ cup	=	4 fluid ounces	=	118 milliliters
1 cup or ½ pint	=	8 fluid ounces	=	250 milliliters
2 cups or 1 pint	=	16 fluid ounces	=	500 milliliters
4 cups or 1 quart	=	32 fluid ounces	=	1,000 milliliters
1 gallon	=	4 liters		

VOLUME (DRY) MEASUREMENTS		
¼ teaspoon	=	1 milliliter
½ teaspoon	=	2 milliliters
¾ teaspoon	=	4 milliliters
1 teaspoon	=	5 milliliters
1 tablespoon	=	15 milliliters
¼ cup	=	59 milliliters
⅓ cup	=	79 milliliters
½ cup	=	118 milliliters
⅔ cup	=	158 milliliters
¾ cup	=	177 milliliters
1 cup	=	225 milliliters
4 cups or 1 quart	=	1 liter
½ gallon	=	2 liters
1 gallon	=	4 liters

With Gratitude

My warmest gratitude to my team. It's a pleasure and a gift to work with such capable men. Leading you all has been a powerful experience. Your strength and unity are what make us such a successful team. I look forward to many more productive years working together. Gracias por todo, mis hombres, each of you has my immense appreciation.

To the profoundly talented food photography team led by Elizabeth Rudge: It was such a compelling experience working with you all. You showed me when skill meets talent, beauty can become explosive.

Elizabeth Rudge, the power you hold in your camera to reflect beauty is astounding. The longer we know each other, the more badass you become. You are the type of leader we should all aspire to be: a deeply talented, fierce, caring, accomplished boss woman who cuts her own path. You endlessly inspire me, friend.

Jenn Elliott Blake, it was such a pleasure to work with you. Your quiet, profound talent should be shared with everyone. I want everything in my life to look as beautiful as it does in your mind.

G. Tyler Hill, your future is so bright; the way you jumped in and styled the hell outta this book was so impressive! Your creativity is a lovely thing to witness.

My deepest gratitude to the *Simple Goodness* families: we all know it takes a village, and you all are an amazing village and community to be a part of. I am so appreciative of everyone for trusting me with your little ones to join in telling my story of care, yummy food, delicious plants, and inclusivity. Working with you and your children made this such a happy project. Thank you so much!

Aguda-Howell family: Afi Howell and Saeed Aguda and Auntie's sweetheart, little Yaqeen Aguda.

Boyagoda-Nikalandawatte family: Raveen Boyagoda and Nishadhi Nikalandawatte and little sweethearts, Reyon and Imaya Boyagoda.

Campbell family: Kerri and Josh and gentle little sweethearts, Dakota and Cash Campbell.

Carey family: Hillary and Brian with their sweet boys, Henry and Gus Carey.

Hunter-Brown family: Leah Hunter and sweet Malaya Brown.

Pineda Muñoz family: Marcos Pineda, Elizabeth Muñoz, and the sweetest baby Marcos Pineda Muñoz Jr.

Polanco-Delgado family: David Polanco and brave, sweet little Fernanda Polanco Delgado.

Salter/Garcia family: Brian Salter and Ivonne Garcia with double sweetness, Naima and Serena Salter.

Sundberg family: Camellia and Paul with sweet little Langston Sundberg.

Townes family: Stacy and Lew, along with their supersweet brood of littles, Tatum, Ethan, and Porter Townes.

Townes family: Walter and Staci and little sweeties, Cooper and Parker Townes.

Yafeu-Pimpleton family: sweet Mama and baby girl Attiyya Yafeu Alleyya Pimpleton.

A heartfelt thank-you to my editor Renee Sedliar. It has been such a pleasure to work with you on this project. From the moment you said yes to *Simple Goodness*, it has been such an exciting team effort; I am so happy and excited to share what we have created. Check us out: two vegan Gen Xers leading the way!

Thanks to my publishing team at Hachette Go, especially Cisca Schreefel; thank you so much for all the very clear directions guiding me through publishing. Nyamekye Waliyaya, genius production director, thank you for making my book beautiful. Diahann Sturgis, the interior sings thank you. Amanda Kain, so lovely to work with you; thank you for everything. Nzinga Temu, editorial assistant, thank you for your work on this project. And the editorial, marketing, and publicity teams, much gratitude.

A note of appreciation to my family.

Thank you to my mother, Niombi. Mom, you are a powerful woman. Watching your half-century dedication to veganism is transcendent. Food is a language of progress and change, and I have had the privilege and awe of observing you steadfastly hold space for change in the way we view and consume food. You owned and operated one of the first plant-based businesses of our time. Through your decades-long work of feeding people, your deep humane and caring understanding of what food is has literally changed the taste of food in our region.

Thank you to my sister, Afi Howell. Being an auntie to your little boy has filled my life with so much fun and joy. Thank you for sharing your baby with me, Sissy.

Thank you to my brother, Ayinde Howell, for letting me bounce all my many thoughts through this process off you.

Auntie's sweet boy, Yaqeen, all your giant zany-kid energy has filled my life with so much joy; I am so lucky I get to be your auntie. It has been the sweetest experience just like you and all your favorite yummy mangoes, sweet bananas ice cream, sprinkle cookies, and chocolate cake all mixed into one! Every day that I get to hang out with you is a yummy adventure of a day filled with toys, fun, friends, bike rides, cartoons, and always more ice cream. Thank you for making auntie's cookbook *Simple Goodness* so special, lovie.

My chef and food service team in white and gray, right to left, front to back:

Led by Chef Marcos Pineda, Maximiliano Pascual (kitchen lead), Willy Hernandez (food preparation lead), Jose Cortez (line cook), Kelvin Argueta (line cook), Oscar Pineda (food production lead), Yovani Hernandez (kitchen maintenance lead), Wilsson Castillo (line cook)

Hospitality service team in black, left to right, front to back:

Led by GM David Polanco, Edilser Pernillo (front-end service lead), Adolfo Barahona (lead front-end host), Rony Osorio (support service lead), Fredy Garcia (bar development lead)

Chef Marcos Pineda, thank you for following me into the depths of veganism. Your willingness to support me as we explore all things nutty, crunchy, and earthy has made it such a pleasure to work with you. I appreciate your constant willingness to grow and learn. I look forward to your continued enthusiasm, dedication, and care as we explore more and more new ways to feed people plants.

Index

Page references in *italics* indicate photographs

Adobo Tofu, Pan-Fried, 181
All-American Kiddo Lunch, *160*, 161
almond milk. *See* milk, plant-based
almonds
  Fresh Cilantro Pesto, 15
apples
  Granny's Apple Crisp à la Mode, 215
  Salted Caramel French Toast with Skillet Spiced Apples, 57
  Sweet Skillet Southern Fried Apples, 32
  Vanilla Caramel Apple Sprinkle Ice-Cream Sammies, 211
applesauce
  Chocolate Chunk Fudge Brownies, 203
Arugula, Eggplant Parmesan with Alfredo Rigatoni and Lemon Olive Oil, 103
Auntie's Meaty Kid-Pleasin' Lasagna, 196, *197*
Auntie's Salted Chocolate Chip Cookies, *204*, 205
Auntie's Secret Strawberry Box Bundt Cake with Lemon Cream Cheese Glaze, *218*, 219
Auntie's Tofu Chili Cornbread, *166*, 167
avocados
  Auntie's Tofu Chili Cornbread, 167
  Baba's Morning Quinoa, 49
  Bacon and Scrambled Egg Tacos, 53
  Blackened Tofu Burgers with Sliced Avocado and Strawberries, 171
  Chicken Burgers with Green Bean Fries, 188
  Chipotle Plant Beef and Bean Tostadas, 123
  Costa Rican Rice and Bean Bowl, 47
  JUST Fried Egg and Cheese Sandwiches, 177
  Macho Burritos, 137
  Papa's Black Beans and Veggie Rice with Sweet Plantains (Maduros), 165
  Plant Beef and Cheese Taquitos with Queso Sauce, 55
  Sausage and Egg Breakfast Burrito, 157
  Shredded or Broken Tofu Tacos, 190
  Spicy Sausage and Hash Browns Tacos, 54
  Tossed Salad Greens with Avocado, Black Beans, and Fresh Coriander Vinaigrette, 107

Baba's Morning Quinoa, *48*, 49
Baba's Smoked Tofu Cold Cuts Sammie, *194*, 195
bacon, vegan
  Bacon and Scrambled Egg Tacos, 53
  Bacon Bits and Bacon Oil, 21
  Bacon Chicken Pasta Bake Leftovers with Garlic Bread, 193
  Bacon Vinaigrette, 22
  Grits and Grease, 64
  Parmesan Herb Croutons, 29
  Salted Caramel French Toast with Skillet Spiced Apples, 57
  Tangy Skillet BBQ Beans, 36
  Tempeh Bacon, 64
  Tofu Bacon, 64
Bacon and Egg Grinder, 92, *93*
Bacon and Scrambled Egg Tacos, 53
Bacon Chicken Pasta Bake Leftovers with Garlic Bread, *192*, 193
Banana Bread and Breakfast Sausage, Yogurt Chia Pudding with, *158*, 159
bananas
  Box Banana Bread, 217
  Chick'n Noodle Soup Leftovers with Cornbread, 179
  Good Morning Good-Belly Strawberry Smoothie, 155
  Strawberry Chia Power Smoothie, 43
BBQ sauce
  BBQ Tofu and Grilled Pineapple Skewers, 110
  Special Sauce, 23
  Tangy Skillet BBQ Beans, 36
BBQ Tofu and Grilled Pineapple Skewers, 110
BBQ Tofu Steaks with Wedged Roasted Yams, *134*, 135
beans and legumes
  Auntie's Tofu Chili Cornbread, 167
  Chipotle Plant Beef and Bean Tostadas, 123
  Citrus Black-Eyed Pea Salad with Sweet Cornbread, 67
  Costa Rican Rice and Bean Bowl, 47
  Macho Burritos, 137
  Papa's Black Beans and Veggie Rice with Sweet Plantains (Maduros), 165
  Tangy Skillet BBQ Beans, 36
  Tossed Salad Greens with Avocado, Black Beans, and Fresh Coriander Vinaigrette, 107
beef, plant-based
  Breakfast Sausage, 60
  Chipotle Plant Beef and Bean Tostadas, 123
  My American Guy Cheeseburger, 139
beets, golden
  Orange Sunrise, 41
biscuits
  Strawberry Shortcake with Skillet Jam and Whipped Cream, 213
  Warm Butter Biscuits, 116
Black Pepper Breading
  Buffalo Portobello Burgers, 141
  Calamari Lettuce Wraps, 71
  Chicken Burgers with Green Bean Fries, 188
  Eggplant Parmesan with Alfredo Rigatoni and Lemon Olive Oil Arugula, 103
  recipe, 16
Black Pepper Chicken Fried Tofu with Cheesy Steamed Broccoli and Carrots, *172*, 173
blackberries
  The Blacker the Berry..., 45
Blackened Tofu Burgers with Sliced Avocado and Strawberries, *170*, 171
Blackened Tofu Grinders, 90, *91*
Blacker the Berry..., The, *44*, 45
Black-Eyed Pea Salad with Sweet Cornbread, Citrus, *66*, 67

blueberries
Fresh Blueberry Icebox Pie, 221
Fruity Chia Yogurt Bowls with Toasted Granola, 51
Bok Choy, Sriracha Meatloaf with Steamed Rice and Sautéed Baby, *132*, 133
Box Banana Bread
recipe, 217
Yogurt Chia Pudding with Banana Bread and Breakfast Sausage, 159
Box Cornbread/Muffins
Chick'n Noodle Soup Leftovers with Cornbread, 179
Citrus Black-Eyed Pea Salad with Sweet Cornbread, 67
recipe, 30
bread
Bacon and Egg Grinder, 92
Blackened Tofu Grinders, 90
Fresh Cilantro Pesto Pasta with Curry Tomato Salad and Pimiento Cheese Toast, 125
Garlic Bread, 33
Herby Cheese Toast, 87
Parmesan Herb Croutons, 29
Salted Caramel French Toast with Skillet Spiced Apples, 57
Spaghetti Ragù and Market Bread, 121
Warm Butter Biscuits, 116
breading
Black Pepper Breading, 16
Mild Black Pepper Breading, 16
Panko Breading, 17
Breakfast Sausage, *56*
in Kiddie Brunch Menu, 150
recipe, 60
Sausage and Egg Breakfast Burrito, 157
broccoli
Black Pepper Chicken Fried Tofu with Cheesy Steamed Broccoli and Carrots, 173
General Tso Cauliflower, 72
Buffalo Portobello Burgers, *140*, 141
Buffalo Sauce, 18
Burger Seasoning, 22
butter, plant-based
Coconut Cheesecake Butter, 32
Garlic Bread, 33
Tajín Butter, 14
Buttery Sweet Peas, 184

Cabbage Lime Slaw, Red, 26
Cake with Lemon Cream Cheese Glaze, Auntie's Secret Strawberry Box Bundt, *218*, 219
Calamari Lettuce Wraps, *70*, 71
cantaloupe
Mama's Golden Melon Milk, 153
Caramel Apple Sprinkle Ice-Cream Sammies, Vanilla, 211
caramel sauce
Sweet Skillet Southern Fried Apples, 32
carrots
Bacon Chicken Pasta Bake Leftovers with Garlic Bread, 193
Black Pepper Chicken Fried Tofu with Cheesy Steamed Broccoli and Carrots, 173
Cauliflower and Yam Bisque, 89
Garden Salad, 117
Hidden Veggie Pasta with Nut-Butter Cracker Sandwiches, 169
Orange Sunrise, 41
Papa's Black Beans and Veggie Rice with Sweet Plantains (Maduros), 165
"Reel Fun Movie Playdate" a.k.a. Mac and Cheese, Corn Dogs, and Dippers, 175
Savory Egg Pancake with Napa Cabbage Slaw and Steamed Rice, 75
Slow Cooker Chick'n Noodle Soup, 115
Veggie or Vegan Chicken Stock, 27
cashews
Wilted Collards, 128
cauliflower
Cauliflower and Yam Bisque, 89
General Tso Cauliflower, 72
Cauliflower and Yam Bisque, *88*, 89
celery
Crockpot Louisiana-Style Gumbo, 85
The Incredible Hulk, 39
"Reel Fun Movie Playdate" a.k.a. Mac and Cheese, Corn Dogs, and Dippers, 175
Slow Cooker Chick'n Noodle Soup, 115
Veggie or Vegan Chicken Stock, 27
chard
Tossed Salad Greens with Avocado, Black Beans, and Fresh Coriander Vinaigrette, 107
Cheddar cheese, vegan
Black Pepper Chicken Fried Tofu with Cheesy Steamed Broccoli and Carrots, 173
Grits and Grease, 64
Hidden Veggie Pasta with Nut-Butter Cracker Sandwiches, 169
JUST Fried Egg and Cheese Sandwiches, 177
Quesadillas and Tajín Butter Street Corn, 199
Simply Good Southern Mac and Cheese, 106
Tame the Hunger Monster Grilled Cheese and Easy Tomato Soup, 163
cheese, plant-based. *See also individual cheese types*
My American Guy Cheeseburger, 139
Pimiento Cheese, 31
Sausage and Egg Breakfast Burrito, 157
chia seeds. *See* Plain Chia Pudding
chicken, plant-based
Chicken Burgers with Green Bean Fries, 188, *189*
Chicken Pasta Bake with Simple Bag Salad and Dressing, 113
Chicken Burgers with Green Bean Fries, 188, *189*
Chicken Pasta Bake with Simple Bag Salad and Dressing, *112*, 113
Chicken Stock, vegan
Auntie's Tofu Chili Cornbread, 167
Cauliflower and Yam Bisque, 89
Chipotle Plant Beef and Bean Tostadas, 123
Crockpot Louisiana-Style Gumbo, 85
recipe, 27
Roasted Mushroom Bisque with Herby Cheese Toast, 87
Roasted Red Pepper Soup, 81
Wild Mushroom Ragù with Parmesan Gnocchi, 101
Chick'n Noodle Soup Leftovers with Cornbread, *178*, 179
Chickpea Salad with Grilled Pita, Middle Eastern–Inspired, *68*, 69
Chili Cornbread, Auntie's Tofu, *166*, 167
Chipotle Dip, 13
Chipotle Plant Beef and Bean Tostadas, *122*, 123
chocolate
Auntie's Salted Chocolate Chip Cookies, 205
Chocolate Chunk Fudge Brownies, 203
Chocolate Chunk Fudge Brownies, *202*, 203
cilantro
Chipotle Plant Beef and Bean Tostadas, 123

Citrus Black-Eyed Pea Salad with Sweet Cornbread, 67
Costa Rican Rice and Bean Bowl, 47
Fresh Cilantro Pesto, 15
Fresh Cilantro Pesto Pasta with Curry Tomato Salad and Pimiento Cheese Toast, 125
Fresh Coriander Vinaigrette, 26
Jalapeño Dip, 12
Kofta Skewers, 109–110
Pico de Gallo, 25
Red Cabbage Lime Slaw, 26
Sun-Dried Tomato Sammie Relish, 20
Citrus Black-Eyed Pea Salad with Sweet Cornbread, *66*, 67
cocoa powder
Chocolate Chunk Fudge Brownies, 203
Coconut Cheesecake Butter, 32
coconut cream/milk
The Blacker the Berry . . ., 45
Cauliflower and Yam Bisque, 89
Coconut Cheesecake Butter, 32
Colby Jack cheese, vegan
Chicken Pasta Bake with Simple Bag Salad and Dressing, 113
Herby Cheese Toast, 87
Macho Burritos, 137
Simply Good Southern Mac and Cheese, 106
coleslaw mix
Red Cabbage Lime Slaw, 26
collards
Creole Tempeh with Wilted Collards and Jasmine Rice, 127–128
Wilted Collards, 128
corn
Hidden Veggie Pasta with Nut-Butter Cracker Sandwiches, 169
Papa's Black Beans and Veggie Rice with Sweet Plantains (Maduros), 165
Quesadillas and Tajín Butter Street Corn, 199
cornbread
Auntie's Tofu Chili Cornbread, 167
Box Cornbread/Muffins, 30
Chick'n Noodle Soup Leftovers with Cornbread, 179
Citrus Black-Eyed Pea Salad with Sweet Cornbread, 67
Corn Dogs, and Dippers, "Reel Fun Movie Playdate" a.k.a. Mac and Cheese, 175
Costa Rican Rice and Bean Bowl, *46*, 47
cream cheese, plant-based
Auntie's Meaty Kid-Pleasin' Lasagna, 196
Auntie's Secret Strawberry Box Bundt Cake with Lemon Cream Cheese Glaze, 219
Coconut Cheesecake Butter, 32
Pimiento Cheese, 31
Simply Good Southern Mac and Cheese, 106
Creamy Chipotle and Fresh Tomato Spaghetti with Grilled Zucchini and Roasted Yams, *130*, 131
Creole Sloppy Joe, *142*, 143
Creole Tempeh with Wilted Collards and Jasmine Rice, *126*, 127–128
Crockpot Louisiana-Style Gumbo, *84*, 85
cucumber
Buffalo Portobello Burgers, 141
The Incredible Hulk, 39
Middle Eastern–Inspired Chickpea Salad with Grilled Pita, 69
Napa Cabbage and Julienned Cucumber Quick Slaw, 77

Dill Dip, 12
dressings
Bacon Vinaigrette, 22
Everyday Italian Salad, 34
Fresh Coriander Vinaigrette, 26
Vegan Ranch, 18

edamame
Buttery Sweet Peas, 184
Lunch Box Ginger Ramen with Scrambled Egg and Steamed Edamame, 187
egg replacements
Baba's Morning Quinoa, 49
Bacon and Egg Grinder, 92
Bacon and Scrambled Egg Tacos, 53
Costa Rican Rice and Bean Bowl, 47
JUST Fried Egg and Cheese Sandwiches, 177
Lunch Box Ginger Ramen with Scrambled Egg and Steamed Edamame, 187
Pan-Fried Eggs, 63
Salted Caramel French Toast with Skillet Spiced Apples, 57
Sausage and Egg Breakfast Burrito, 157
Savory Egg Pancake with Napa Cabbage Slaw and Steamed Rice, 75
Eggplant Parmesan with Alfredo Rigatoni and Lemon Olive Oil Arugula, 103, *103*
espresso powder
Chocolate Chunk Fudge Brownies, 203
Everyday Italian Salad, 34

French Onion Soup with Herby Cheese Toast, *82*, 83
Fresh Blueberry Icebox Pie, *220*, 221
Fresh Cilantro Pesto
Baba's Morning Quinoa, 49
Fresh Cilantro Pesto Pasta with Curry Tomato Salad and Pimiento Cheese Toast, 125
recipe, 15
Fresh Cilantro Pesto Pasta with Curry Tomato Salad and Pimiento Cheese Toast, *124*, 125
Fresh Coriander Vinaigrette
recipe, 26
Tossed Salad Greens with Avocado, Black Beans, and, 107
Fresh Herb Oil, 20
Fruity Chia Yogurt Bowls with Toasted Granola, *50*, 51
Funfetti Pancakes, 151

Garden Salad, 117
garlic, roasted
Dill Dip, 12
Fresh Cilantro Pesto, 15
Mild Black Pepper Breading, 16
Yogurt Tahini Sauce, 15
Garlic Bread, 33
Bacon Chicken Pasta Bake Leftovers with Garlic Bread, 193
General Tso Cauliflower, 72, *73*
Ginger Ramen with Scrambled Egg and Steamed Edamame, Lunch Box, *186*, 187
Gnocchi, Wild Mushroom Ragù with Parmesan, *100*,101
gochujang
General Tso Cauliflower, 72
Good Morning Good-Belly Strawberry Smoothie, *154*, 155
Granny's Apple Crisp à la Mode, 215
Granola, Fruity Chia Yogurt Bowls with Toasted, *50*, 51
green beans
All-American Kiddo Lunch, 161
Chicken Burgers with Green Bean Fries, 188

green onions
Crockpot Louisiana-Style Gumbo, 85
Fresh Cilantro Pesto Pasta with Curry Tomato Salad and Pimiento Cheese Toast, 125
Lunch Box Ginger Ramen with Scrambled Egg and Steamed Edamame, 187
Napa Cabbage and Julienned Cucumber Quick Slaw, 77
Red Cabbage Lime Slaw, 26
Savory Egg Pancake with Napa Cabbage Slaw and Steamed Rice, 75
greens
Buffalo Portobello Burgers, 141
Everyday Italian Salad, 34
Macho Burritos, 137
Grinder Salad, 90
Grits and Grease, *62*, 64
Gyro Spice Blend, 28

hash browns, frozen
Sausage and Egg Breakfast Burrito, 157
Hello Sunshine Quinoa Tabbouleh, *78*, 79
Herby Cheese Toast
French Onion Soup with Herby Cheese Toast, 83
recipe, 87
Roasted Mushroom Bisque with Herby Cheese Toast, 87
Hidden Veggie Pasta with Nut-Butter Cracker Sandwiches, *168*, 169

ice cream, plant-based
Granny's Apple Crisp à la Mode, 215
Strawberry Shortcake Ice-Cream Bars, 223–224
Vanilla Caramel Apple Sprinkle Ice-Cream Sammies, 211
Incredible Hulk, The, *38*, 39
ingredients, stocking, 4, 6, 8

Jalapeño Dip, 12
Jasmine Rice, 128
JUST Fried Egg and Cheese Sandwiches, *176*, 177

kale
The Incredible Hulk, 39
Tossed Salad Greens with Avocado, Black Beans, and Fresh Coriander Vinaigrette, 107
kiwis
Fruity Chia Yogurt Bowls with Toasted Granola, 51
Kofta Skewers, *108*, 109–110

Lasagna, Auntie's Meaty Kid Pleasin', 196
lemon zest
Auntie's Secret Strawberry Box Bundt Cake with Lemon Cream Cheese Glaze, 219
lemons/lemon juice
Baba's Morning Quinoa, 49
Pepper Pot Pickled Onions, 25
Strawberry Skillet Jam, 30
lettuce
Baba's Smoked Tofu Cold Cuts Sammie, 195
Bacon and Egg Grinder, 92
Chipotle Plant Beef and Bean Tostadas, 123
Garden Salad, 117
Grinder Salad, 90
My American Guy Cheeseburger, 139
Oyster Mushroom Po' Boys, 145
Portobello Gyros, 95
Shredded or Broken Tofu Tacos, 190
Tofu Bacon, Lettuce, and Tomato Sammie, 97
limes/lime juice
Costa Rican Rice and Bean Bowl, 47
Middle Eastern–Inspired Chickpea Salad with Grilled Pita, 69
Red Cabbage Lime Slaw, 26
Lunch Box Ginger Ramen with Scrambled Egg and Steamed Edamame, *186*, 187

Macho Burritos, *136*, 137
Mama Made Pepperoni Pizza Pockets with Buttery Sweet Peas, *182*, 183
Mama's Golden Melon Milk, *152*, 153
mangos
Chick'n Noodle Soup Leftovers with Cornbread, 179
Fruity Chia Yogurt Bowls with Toasted Granola, 51
Marinara Sauce, 19
meat, plant-based. *See also* beef, plant-based; chicken, plant-based; sausage, vegan
Auntie's Meaty Kid-Pleasin' Lasagna, 196
Creole Sloppy Joe, 143
Kofta Skewers, 109–110
Quesadillas and Tajín Butter Street Corn, 199
Spaghetti Ragù and Market Bread, 121
Sriracha Meatloaf with Steamed Rice and Sautéed Baby Bok Choy, 133
metric conversions, 225–227
Middle Eastern–Inspired Chickpea Salad with Grilled Pita, *68*, *69*
Mild Black Pepper Breading, 16
Milk, Mama's Golden Melon, *152*, 153
mint
Fresh Cilantro Pesto, 15
Gyro Spice Blend, 28
Sweet Chili Sauce, 19
Yogurt Tahini Sauce, 15
mizuna
Tossed Salad Greens with Avocado, Black Beans, and Fresh Coriander Vinaigrette, 107
mozzarella, vegan
Auntie's Meaty Kid-Pleasin' Lasagna, 196
Chicken Pasta Bake with Simple Bag Salad and Dressing, 113
Eggplant Parmesan with Alfredo Rigatoni and Lemon Olive Oil Arugula, 103
Mama Made Pepperoni Pizza Pockets with Buttery Sweet Peas, 183
Quesadillas and Tajín Butter Street Corn, 199
mushrooms
Auntie's Meaty Kid-Pleasin' Lasagna, 196
Buffalo Portobello Burgers, 141
Calamari Lettuce Wraps, 71
Chicken Pasta Bake with Simple Bag Salad and Dressing, 113
My American Guy Cheeseburger, 139
Portobello Gyros, 95
Roasted Mushroom Bisque with Herby Cheese Toast, 87
Slow Cooker Chick'n Noodle Soup, 115
Tofu Egg Scramble, 58
Veggie and Sausage Kebabs, 111
Veggie or Vegan Chicken Stock, 27
Wild Mushroom Ragù with Parmesan Gnocchi, 101
My American Guy Cheeseburger, *138*, 139

My Sweet Georgia Peach, *206*, 207–208, *209*

Napa Cabbage and Julienned Cucumber Quick Slaw, 77
Nut-Butter Cracker Sammies, 169
nutritional yeast
Wilted Collards, 128

oats
Granny's Apple Crisp à la Mode, 215
okra
Crockpot Louisiana-Style Gumbo, 85
onions
French Onion Soup with Herby Cheese Toast, 83
Pepper Pot Pickled Onions, 25
Sautéed Onions, 23
orange juice
The Blacker the Berry…, 45
Good Morning Good-Belly Strawberry Smoothie, 155
My Sweet Georgia Peach, 207–208
Strawberry Chia Power Smoothie, 43
Orange Sunrise, *40*, 41
oranges
Bacon Chicken Pasta Bake Leftovers with Garlic Bread, 193
JUST Fried Egg and Cheese Sandwiches, 177
Pico de Gallo, 25
"Reel Fun Movie Playdate" a.k.a. Mac and Cheese, Corn Dogs, and Dippers, 175
oregano
Fresh Herb Oil, 20
Gyro Spice Blend, 28
Panko Breading, 17
Oyster Mushroom Po' Boys, *144*, 145

Pajamas and Pancakes Brunch Party! 150
Pan-Fried Adobo Tofu, *180*, 181
Pan-Fried Cajun Butter Blackened Tofu, *104*, 105
Blackened Tofu Burgers with Sliced Avocado and Strawberries, 171
Blackened Tofu Grinders, 90
Pan-Fried Eggs, *62*, 63
Panko Breading, 17
pantry items, 4, 6, 8
Papa's Black Beans
Macho Burritos, 137
and Veggie Rice with Sweet Plantains (Maduros), 165
Papa's Black Beans and Veggie Rice with Sweet Plantains (Maduros), *164*, 165
Papa's Sammie Sauce
Baba's Smoked Tofu Cold Cuts Sammie, 195
Bacon and Egg Grinder, 92
Blackened Tofu Grinders, 90
recipe, 13
Tofu Bacon, Lettuce, and Tomato Sammie, 97
Parmesan cheese, vegan
Auntie's Meaty Kid-Pleasin' Lasagna, 196
Bacon and Scrambled Egg Tacos, 53
BBQ Tofu Steaks with Wedged Roasted Yams, 135
Chicken Pasta Bake with Simple Bag Salad and Dressing, 113
Chipotle Plant Beef and Bean Tostadas, 123
Creamy Chipotle and Fresh Tomato Spaghetti with Grilled Zucchini and Roasted Yams, 131
Eggplant Parmesan with Alfredo Rigatoni and Lemon Olive Oil Arugula, 103
Everyday Italian Salad, 34
Fresh Cilantro Pesto, 15
Fresh Cilantro Pesto Pasta with Curry Tomato Salad and Pimiento Cheese Toast, 125
Garlic Bread, 33
Parmesan Herb Croutons, 29
Tajín Butter, 14
Wedged Roasted Yams, 24
Wild Mushroom Ragù with Parmesan Gnocchi, 101
Parmesan Herb Croutons
Everyday Italian Salad, 34
recipe, 29
Roasted Red Pepper Soup, 81
pasta
Auntie's Meaty Kid-Pleasin' Lasagna, 196
Bacon Chicken Pasta Bake Leftovers with Garlic Bread, 193
Chicken Pasta Bake with Simple Bag Salad and Dressing, 113
Creamy Chipotle and Fresh Tomato Spaghetti with Grilled Zucchini and Roasted Yams, 131
Eggplant Parmesan with Alfredo Rigatoni and Lemon Olive Oil Arugula, 103
Fresh Cilantro Pesto Pasta with Curry Tomato Salad and Pimiento Cheese Toast, 125
Hidden Veggie Pasta with Nut-Butter Cracker Sandwiches, 169
Lunch Box Ginger Ramen with Scrambled Egg and Steamed Edamame, 187
Simply Good Southern Mac and Cheese, 106
Slow Cooker Chick'n Noodle Soup, 115
Spaghetti Ragù and Market Bread, 121
Peach, My Sweet Georgia, *206*, 207–208
peanut butter
Nut-Butter Cracker Sammies, 169
peas
Buttery Sweet Peas, 184
Hidden Veggie Pasta with Nut-Butter Cracker Sandwiches, 169
Mama Made Pepperoni Pizza Pockets with Buttery Sweet Peas, 183
Papa's Black Beans and Veggie Rice with Sweet Plantains (Maduros), 165
Pepper Pot Pickled Onions, 25
Pepperoni Pizza Pockets with Buttery Sweet Peas, Mama Made, *182*, 183
peppers, bell
Auntie's Tofu Chili Cornbread, 167
Citrus Black-Eyed Pea Salad with Sweet Cornbread, 67
Costa Rican Rice and Bean Bowl, 47
Creole Sloppy Joe, 143
Crockpot Louisiana-Style Gumbo, 85
Kofta Skewers, 109–110
Quesadillas and Tajín Butter Street Corn, 199
Roasted Red Pepper Soup, 81
Shredded or Broken Tofu Tacos, 190
Tangy Skillet BBQ Beans, 36
Tofu Egg Scramble, 58
Veggie and Sausage Kebabs, 111
peppers, hot
Calamari Lettuce Wraps, 71
Chipotle Dip, 13
Chipotle Plant Beef and Bean Tostadas, 123

peppers, hot (*continue*)
Citrus Black-Eyed Pea Salad with Sweet Cornbread, 67
Creamy Chipotle and Fresh Tomato Spaghetti with Grilled Zucchini and Roasted Yams, 131
Everyday Italian Salad, 34
Fresh Cilantro Pesto, 15
Fresh Cilantro Pesto Pasta with Curry Tomato Salad and Pimiento Cheese Toast, 125
Hello Sunshine Quinoa Tabbouleh, 79
Jalapeño Dip, 12
Kofta Skewers, 109–110
Napa Cabbage and Julienned Cucumber Quick Slaw, 77
Pepper Pot Pickled Onions, 25
Pico de Gallo, 25
Pimiento Cheese, 31
Red Cabbage Lime Slaw, 26
Tajín Butter, 14
Pico de Gallo, 25
pies
Fresh Blueberry Icebox Pie, 221
My Sweet Georgia Peach, 207–208
Pimiento Cheese, 31
pineapple
BBQ Tofu and Grilled Pineapple Skewers, 110
The Blacker the Berry..., 45
Hello Sunshine Quinoa Tabbouleh, 79
Pizza Pockets with Buttery Sweet Peas, Mama Made Pepperoni, *182*, 183
Plain Chia Pudding
The Blacker the Berry..., 45
Fruity Chia Yogurt Bowls with Toasted Granola, 51
Good Morning Good-Belly Strawberry Smoothie, 155
recipe, 33
Strawberry Chia Power Smoothie, 43
Yogurt Chia Pudding with Banana Bread and Breakfast Sausage, 159
Plant Beef and Cheese Taquitos with Queso Sauce, *52*, 55
plantains
Costa Rican Rice and Bean Bowl, 47
Papa's Black Beans and Veggie Rice with Sweet Plantains (Maduros), 165
Tostones, 35
pork, plant-based, suggestions for, 6
Portobello Burgers, Buffalo, *140*, 141
Portobello Gyros, *94*, 95
potato gnocchi
Wild Mushroom Ragù with Parmesan Gnocchi, 101
potatoes
Skillet Breakfast Potatoes, 59
Spicy Sausage and Hash Browns Tacos, 54
provolone, vegan
Black Pepper Chicken Fried Tofu with Cheesy Steamed Broccoli and Carrots, 173
Eggplant Parmesan with Alfredo Rigatoni and Lemon Olive Oil Arugula, 103
Simply Good Southern Mac and Cheese, 106
puff pastry
Mama Made Pepperoni Pizza Pockets with Buttery Sweet Peas, 183

Quesadillas and Tajín Butter Street Corn, *198*, 199
quinoa
Baba's Morning Quinoa, 49
Hello Sunshine Quinoa Tabbouleh, 79

Red Cabbage Lime Slaw, 26
"Reel Fun Movie Playdate" a.k.a. Mac and Cheese, Corn Dogs, and Dippers, *174*, 175
rice
Costa Rican Rice and Bean Bowl, 47
Creole Tempeh with Wilted Collards and Jasmine Rice, 127–128
Crockpot Louisiana-Style Gumbo, 85
General Tso Cauliflower, 72
Jasmine Rice, 128
Macho Burritos, 137
Papa's Black Beans and Veggie Rice with Sweet Plantains (Maduros), 165
Spanish Rice, 24
Sriracha Meatloaf with Steamed Rice and Sautéed Baby Bok Choy, 133
Roasted Mushroom Bisque with Herby Cheese Toast, *86*, 87
Roasted Red Pepper Soup, *80*, 81

salads
Chicken Pasta Bake with Simple Bag Salad and Dressing, 113
Citrus Black-Eyed Pea Salad with Sweet Cornbread, 67
Everyday Italian Salad, 34
Garden Salad, 117
Grinder Salad, 90
Middle Eastern–Inspired Chickpea Salad with Grilled Pita, 69
Tossed Salad Greens with Avocado, Black Beans, and Fresh Coriander Vinaigrette, 107
Salted Caramel French Toast with Skillet Spiced Apples, 57
sauces, suggestions for, 8. *See also individual sauces*
sausage, vegan
Crockpot Louisiana-Style Gumbo, 85
Plant Beef and Cheese Taquitos with Queso Sauce, 55
Sausage and Egg Breakfast Burrito, 157
Spicy Sausage and Hash Browns Tacos, 54
Veggie and Sausage Kebabs, 111
Yogurt Chia Pudding with Banana Bread and Breakfast Sausage, 159
Sausage and Egg Breakfast Burrito, *156*, 157
Sautéed Onions, 23
Savory Egg Pancake with Napa Cabbage Slaw and Steamed Rice, *74*, 75
seitan
Chicken Pasta Bake with Simple Bag Salad and Dressing, 113
shallots
Creole Tempeh with Wilted Collards and Jasmine Rice, 127–128
Fresh Herb Oil, 20
Shortcake Ice-Cream Bars, Strawberry, 223–224
Shredded or Broken Tofu Tacos, 190, *191*
Simply Good Southern Mac and Cheese, *104*, 106
Skillet Breakfast Potatoes, *56*, 59
Slow Cooker Chick'n Noodle Soup, 115, *118–119*
smoothies
Blacker the Berry..., The, *44*, 45
Good Morning Good-Belly Strawberry Smoothie, 155
Strawberry Chia Power Smoothie, *42*
Spaghetti Ragù and Market Bread, *120*, 121

Spanish Rice, 24
Special Sauce, 23
Spicy Sausage and Hash Browns Tacos, *52*, 54
spinach
  Auntie's Meaty Kid-Pleasin' Lasagna, 196
  Baba's Morning Quinoa, 49
  Chicken Pasta Bake with Simple Bag Salad and Dressing, 113
  The Incredible Hulk, 39
  Tossed Salad Greens with Avocado, Black Beans, and Fresh Coriander Vinaigrette, 107
sriracha
  Lunch Box Ginger Ramen with Scrambled Egg and Steamed Edamame, 187
  Savory Egg Pancake with Napa Cabbage Slaw and Steamed Rice, 75
  Sriracha Meatloaf with Steamed Rice and Sautéed Baby Bok Choy, 133
Sriracha Meatloaf with Steamed Rice and Sautéed Baby Bok Choy, *132*, 133
strawberries
  Auntie's Secret Strawberry Box Bundt Cake with Lemon Cream Cheese Glaze, 219
  Blackened Tofu Burgers with Sliced Avocado and Strawberries, 171
  Good Morning Good-Belly Strawberry Smoothie, 155
  Strawberry Chia Power Smoothie, 43
  Strawberry Shortcake Ice-Cream Bars, 223–224
  Strawberry Shortcake with Skillet Jam and Whipped Cream, 213
Strawberry Chia Power Smoothie, *42*, 43
Strawberry Shortcake Ice-Cream Bars, *222*, 223
Strawberry Shortcake with Skillet Jam and Whipped Cream, *212*, 213
Strawberry Skillet Jam, 30
Sun-Dried Tomato Sammie Relish, 20
Sweet Chili Sauce, 19
sweet potatoes. *See* yams
Sweet Skillet Southern Fried Apples, 32

Tabasco Aioli, 14
Tabbouleh, Hello Sunshine Quinoa, 79
Taco Seasoning, 17
tacos
  Bacon and Scrambled Egg Tacos, 53
  Plant Beef and Cheese Taquitos with Queso Sauce, 55
  Shredded or Broken Tofu Tacos, 190
  Spicy Sausage and Hash Browns Tacos, 54
Tahini Sauce, Yogurt, 15
Tajín Butter, 14
tamari sauce
  BBQ Tofu Steaks with Wedged Roasted Yams, 135
  Creole Tempeh with Wilted Collards and Jasmine Rice, 127–128
  French Onion Soup with Herby Cheese Toast, 83
  Lunch Box Ginger Ramen with Scrambled Egg and Steamed Edamame, 187
  Pan-Fried Cajun Butter Blackened Tofu, 105
  Savory Egg Pancake with Napa Cabbage Slaw and Steamed Rice, 75
  Sweet Chili Sauce, 19
  Tofu Egg Scramble, 58
Tame the Hunger Monster Grilled Cheese and Easy Tomato Soup, *162*, 163
Tangy Skillet BBQ Beans, 36
tempeh
  Creole Tempeh with Wilted Collards and Jasmine Rice, 127–128
  Tempeh Bacon, *62*, 64
Tempeh Bacon, *62*, 64
tofu
  Auntie's Tofu Chili Cornbread, 167
  Baba's Morning Quinoa, 49
  Baba's Smoked Tofu Cold Cuts Sammie, 195
  BBQ Tofu and Grilled Pineapple Skewers, 110
  BBQ Tofu Steaks with Wedged Roasted Yams, 135
  Black Pepper Chicken Fried Tofu with Cheesy Steamed Broccoli and Carrots, 173
  Blackened Tofu Burgers with Sliced Avocado and Strawberries, 171
  Pan-Fried Adobo Tofu, 181
  Pan-Fried Cajun Butter Blackened Tofu, 105
  Quesadillas and Tajín Butter Street Corn, 199
  Shredded or Broken Tofu Tacos, 190
  Slow Cooker Chick'n Noodle Soup, 115
  Tofu Egg Scramble, 58
tofu, mesquite
  Bacon and Egg Grinder, 92
  Bacon and Scrambled Egg Tacos, 53
  Bacon Bits and Bacon Oil, 21
  Chicken Pasta Bake with Simple Bag Salad and Dressing, 113
  Salted Caramel French Toast with Skillet Spiced Apples, 57
  Tangy Skillet BBQ Beans, 36
  Tofu Bacon, 64
  Tofu Bacon, Lettuce, and Tomato Sammie, 97
Tofu Bacon, *62*, 64
Tofu Bacon, Lettuce, and Tomato Sammie, *96*, 97
Tofu Egg Scramble, *56*, 58
tomato juice
  Spanish Rice, 24
tomato sauce
  Auntie's Meaty Kid-Pleasin' Lasagna, 196
  Auntie's Tofu Chili Cornbread, 167
  Chipotle Plant Beef and Bean Tostadas, 123
  Hidden Veggie Pasta with Nut-Butter Cracker Sandwiches, 169
  Spaghetti Ragù and Market Bread, 121
Tomato Soup, Tame the Hunger Monster Grilled Cheese and Easy, 163
tomatoes
  Auntie's Meaty Kid-Pleasin' Lasagna, 196
  Auntie's Tofu Chili Cornbread, 167
  Baba's Smoked Tofu Cold Cuts Sammie, 195
  Blackened Tofu Grinders, 90
  Chicken Pasta Bake with Simple Bag Salad and Dressing, 113
  Chipotle Plant Beef and Bean Tostadas, 123
  Citrus Black-Eyed Pea Salad with Sweet Cornbread, 67
  Costa Rican Rice and Bean Bowl, 47
  Creamy Chipotle and Fresh Tomato Spaghetti with Grilled Zucchini and Roasted Yams, 131
  Creole Sloppy Joe, 143

tomatoes (*continue*)
Creole Tempeh with Wilted Collards and Jasmine Rice, 127–128
tomatoes (*continued*)
Crockpot Louisiana-Style Gumbo, 85
Everyday Italian Salad, 34
Fresh Cilantro Pesto Pasta with Curry Tomato Salad and Pimiento Cheese Toast, 125
Garden Salad, 117
Hello Sunshine Quinoa Tabbouleh, 79
JUST Fried Egg and Cheese Sandwiches, 177
Marinara Sauce, 19
Middle Eastern–Inspired Chickpea Salad with Grilled Pita, 69
My American Guy Cheeseburger, 139
Oyster Mushroom Po' Boys, 145
Papa's Black Beans and Veggie Rice with Sweet Plantains (Maduros), 165
Pico de Gallo, 25
Portobello Gyros, 95
Roasted Red Pepper Soup, 81
Shredded or Broken Tofu Tacos, 190
Spaghetti Ragù and Market Bread, 121
Sun-Dried Tomato Sammie Relish, 20
Tofu Bacon, Lettuce, and Tomato Sammie, 97
Wild Mushroom Ragù with Parmesan Gnocchi, 101
tortillas
Macho Burritos, 137
Plant Beef and Cheese Taquitos with Queso Sauce, 55
Quesadillas and Tajín Butter Street Corn, 199
Sausage and Egg Breakfast Burrito, 157
Shredded or Broken Tofu Tacos, 190
Spicy Sausage and Hash Browns Tacos, 54
Tossed Salad Greens with Avocado, Black Beans, and Fresh Coriander Vinaigrette, *104*, 107
Tostones, 35

Vanilla Caramel Apple Sprinkle Ice-Cream Sammies, *210*, 211
Vegan Ranch, 18
Veggie and Sausage Kebabs, 111
Veggie Stock
Cauliflower and Yam Bisque, 89
Chipotle Plant Beef and Bean Tostadas, 123
Crockpot Louisiana-Style Gumbo, 85
recipe, 27
Shredded or Broken Tofu Tacos, 190
Slow Cooker Chick'n Noodle Soup, 115
Wild Mushroom Ragù with Parmesan Gnocchi, 101

Warm Butter Biscuits, 116, *118–119*
Wedged Roasted Yams, 24
BBQ Tofu Steaks with, 135
Whipped Cream, Strawberry Shortcake with Skillet Jam and, 213
Wild Mushroom Ragù with Parmesan Gnocchi, *100*, 101
Wilted Collards, 128
wine, red
French Onion Soup with Herby Cheese Toast, 83
Marinara Sauce, 19
Wild Mushroom Ragù with Parmesan Gnocchi, 101
wine, white
Creole Tempeh with Wilted Collards and Jasmine Rice, 127–128
Tangy Skillet BBQ Beans, 36

yams
BBQ Tofu Steaks with Wedged Roasted Yams, 135
Cauliflower and Yam Bisque, 89
Wedged Roasted Yams, 24
yogurt, plant-based
Baba's Morning Quinoa, 49
Fruity Chia Yogurt Bowls with Toasted Granola, 51
Yogurt Chia Pudding with Banana Bread and Breakfast Sausage, 159
Yogurt Tahini Sauce, 15

zucchini
Creamy Chipotle and Fresh Tomato Spaghetti with Grilled Zucchini and Roasted Yams, 131
Savory Egg Pancake with Napa Cabbage Slaw and Steamed Rice, 75